# A
# REPURPOSED
# LIFE

# A
# REPURPOSED
# LIFE

# RONNI KAHN

with Jessica Chapnik Kahn

**murdoch books**

Sydney | London

Published in 2020 by Murdoch Books,
an imprint of Allen & Unwin

Murdoch Books Australia
83 Alexander Street, Crows Nest NSW 2065
Phone: +61 (0)2 8425 0100
murdochbooks.com.au
info@murdochbooks.com.au

Murdoch Books UK
Ormond House, 26–27 Boswell Street, London WC1N 3JZ
Phone: +44 (0) 20 8785 5995
murdochbooks.co.uk
info@murdochbooks.co.uk

A catalogue record for this
book is available from the
NATIONAL LIBRARY OF AUSTRALIA National Library of Australia

A catalogue record for this book is available from the British Library
ISBN 978 1 76052 590 3 Australia
ISBN 978 1 91163 294 8 UK

Cover design by Trisha Garner
Text design by Susanne Geppert
Cover photography by Andrew Finlayson/*Australian Gourmet Traveller*/
Bauer Media Pty Limited/bauersyndication.com.au
Typeset by Midland Typesetters, Australia
Printed and bound in Australia by Griffin Press

Grateful acknowledgement is made for permission to reprint quoted material from
*How to Cure a Fanatic* by Amos Oz. Published by Vintage. Reprinted by permission
of The Random House Group Limited. © 2012

'Safi, your book should be called *In My Heart* . . .'
—Lev Vishnu Kahn (three years old)


*For my grandchildren, who light up my life with their profound wisdom and innocence. You are my everything. You are my heart.*

'All of us are blessed with capabilities and skills, but it is how we utilise them for the benefit of mankind which is most important.'
—Sri Sakthi Narayani Amma

# CONTENTS

## PART 4: OZHARVEST

## PART 5: TRUE CALLING

# PREFACE

At 51 years of age, I found myself packing up my partner's things in a mad, cathartic frenzy. We were over. It had been a long time coming. For seven years I'd lived a vacuous life with this man. I hadn't known it then, but I knew it now. I was packing and crying (because of my mistakes and humiliation), packing and laughing (because it was strangely energising), and with every book, CD and tie that I hurled into a box, I let myself feel how badly I wanted something more from my life. And I wanted it now. I'd squandered a lot of time. But I was finally free to be the person I wanted to be, not the person I had been.

Until this point in time, I had thought I was content and fulfilled. But all of a sudden, every part of my body, every one of my cells, wanted to know what it felt like to do something beyond surviving, beyond making money, beyond pleasure and travel and a beautiful home and a partner and lovely things. I wanted to feel something beyond 'happy'. That day, staring at the remains of my relationship, reduced to useless boxes of belongings, I asked myself this question: is this life of mine good for me and is it doing good for others?

These days, I'm often asked what the exact ingredients are to a 'purpose-filled' life. People want to know the steps I took to arrive at this point, where I find my energy, how to get what they think I have. They want to know how to find passion and purpose, how to wake up feeling complete, how OzHarvest became what it is. All I can tell you for sure is that the day I really started questioning what was meaningful to me, everything changed.

Many of us, myself included, love a good list or recipe—something to follow to make sure everything turns out as it should. But if my life was a recipe, the ingredients would be 'a bit of this' and 'a bit of that'. All in good measure, but nothing precise or calculated. The disclaimer would be, *You don't need all the ingredients to make this dish.* If you don't have flour, if you don't have butter, it doesn't mean you can't bake a cake. It all depends on how you define cake! I was brought up to value improvisation when creating recipes. My mother taught me that; she wasn't daunted by rules. She'd try this and that, and then she'd taste it—that's an important bit. And it always turned out beautifully. So I've often made things up. Not made do. Making do feels like a compromise. But making up is creative. Life throws us mysterious ingredients. If we are brave enough to put the recipe aside and experiment, it's right there that things get interesting.

Knowing how to improvise missing ingredients perhaps partly answers the question of how I've done what I've done and how I continue to do what I do. Because it's a sure thing that I've never had the ingredients you 'need' to create the life I lead now. Never have I been considered particularly capable, beautiful, funny or popular. I was never academic, nor particularly smart. I wasn't the one with 'personality' or 'talent'. Never in my wildest dreams could I have imagined starting a charity or a significant organisation, leading people or speaking in public. These days, I'm validated in many ways for the things I do, but there was a time in my life when the things I was good at were completely invisible, or they were taken for granted. There was a time when I saw myself as a little mouse in the corner of the rooms I inhabited. I had no sense that I had the capacity to do anything great, and yet I know now that I have played a part in creating some great things. Therefore, if a person like me—a person missing so many ingredients in the recipe for making 'something great'—can do these things, then anyone can.

What is truly mysterious to me is how I arrived at the point of penning a book. But here I am, venturing forward, ready to share this journey with you.

# PART 1

# SOUTH AFRICA

# CHAPTER 1

# APARTNESS

I may as well set the record straight right from the get-go that my name really is just Ronni. Not Veronica. Not Rhonda. Not Rona. And not Ronnie with an 'e'. It's not hidden inside any other name. After my two older sisters, my father had wanted a boy very badly. Ronni was the name he had chosen for that boy, and when I was born, the name Ronni remained. I liked it. I felt interesting. But it confused people too. Growing up, I always had the sense that my name challenged people somehow, because a girl was standing in front of them, not a boy. In my early business life, people often sounded a little taken aback when I was the voice behind the name Ronni Kahn. They were expecting to find the expertise of a respectable man whose full name, perhaps, was Ronald. (Or an Indian prince called Raj Khan!)

Despite me being an unexpected third daughter, my parents adored me, as did my sisters, Pamela and Margie. Being ten years younger than Pam and five years younger than Margie, I was the spoilt baby of the household and, I like to think, my father's favourite. (Sorry, sisters!) Even then, I had a sense that I had him wrapped around my little finger. Maybe because I was the baby, he spoiled me more than he did my sisters. He'd often get in trouble from my mother for indulging me with chocolate bars and other treats. He used to lovingly call me his *feigele*, which means 'little bird' in Yiddish. My parents had grown up in small villages in South Africa that spoke English and Afrikaans, the two official languages of the South Africa of my childhood. But their parents were European immigrants who spoke to them in Yiddish, so we grew up speaking English, with Yiddish words smattered throughout. We all learnt Afrikaans at school, because it was compulsory, but I never connected with that language.

I don't know whether there is any correlation with my boyish name, but I was instantly a tomboy. Maybe I wanted to play this out for my dad in some way, to try to live up to my idea of the name. He certainly went all out to provide me with the stereotypical boy things of the time. He would build go-carts out of soapboxes for me and the neighbourhood boys. This was not what the other little girls on our street were doing. I had so many smashes and crashes. I broke my arm and scraped myself continually, climbing trees with the boys. I'd pee standing up in the hydrangea bushes, because that's what the boys were doing. The tomboy thing really worked for me; I had so much fun.

But when night-time came around, it wasn't so much fun. I was so afraid of the darkness in my room that, even now, just thinking about it, I can feel the fear in my body. To deal with this crippling fear, my father gave me his wooden walking stick to put beside my bed. That stick really helped. If I had bad thoughts, I could always 'touch wood'. It worked. The smooth smell of the wood, the feeling of my father's strength; for a few seconds or minutes at least, they made everything okay. I know it's a common thing for kids to be afraid of the dark, nothing unusual there. But I tell this story because I think there is something a little sinister in this memory. This stick was also there in case I needed to use it. It was a real weapon, one that a small child could use against a genuine threat. Outside my window, on my street, in my suburb and in my country, things were pretty ruthless. Every night, I was prepared, with my whole mind, to use that stick. This was life under apartheid in South Africa.

It's hard to believe you can grow up with brutal injustice in front of your face and carry on comfortably living your life. You can. To this day, my sisters and I struggle to believe that we grew up with that numbness. There are covert injustices everywhere we look in our lives, within our countries and within our local environments. But under apartheid, in 1950s South Africa, there was nothing covert about the injustice. We grew up seeing everything, and noticing nothing at all. When you are born within a system, you take it as a given. You don't have another reference point.

Apartheid is the Afrikaans word for 'apartness', and in a nutshell that is exactly what apartheid was—a system to keep us all separate, according to the colour of our skin. Although racial segregation has a long and devastating history in South Africa, in 1948, a few years before I was born, apartheid became enshrined in the law. Supported and institutionalised by the National Party government, this rigid racial policy officially mandated the segregation of all racial groups in South Africa. Although white people were the minority, apartheid espoused white supremacy, and set up all its laws to benefit only white people. Any race that wasn't white was repressed in the most brutal way. If you were black or Asian or mixed race, you were forced to mingle exclusively among your own racial group; you were evicted from your home and obliged to live separately from all other racial groups. You were forced to comply with curfews. You were required to use separate buses and trains from whites, walk through separate doors from whites, have no friends who were white, have no ability to vote, have no sexual relationship across racial lines. You were offered no proper education. The legislation was absolute and had fearsome, state-authorised, institutionally controlled consequences to punish any who disobeyed. It dictated all our lives, whether we were benefiting, suffering or indifferent.

One of my strongest childhood memories is seeing clusters of black people on street corners. I never knew what they were doing there. As an adult, looking back, I suppose street corners were all they had. They had no spaces of their own in which to congregate. If they were looking for work, they had nowhere to go in the 'all-white' suburbs. They just had to gather around and sit on kerbsides, because there was nowhere else for them to sit. If they needed to buy something—such as food—they had to find the odd corner shop with a side door that said 'Non-Whites'. God forbid they might walk through the same door we did! This was absolutely against the law. They had to find their 'Non-White' doors and their 'Non-White' buses and their 'Non-White' trains. Their homes were hours away from ours, and their children were somewhere 'out there' with their grandparents. They were made socially separate from us in every way possible. If I close my eyes, I can still see their forlorn faces on those street corners, can still hear the incredible melody in their voices.

I consider myself lucky to have had parents and grandparents who believed all people were equal. They had come from a religious Jewish background of rabbis and scholars and had been brought up with pristine values. But it was complex, because even if you believed in equality, it was whittled away by a system that didn't allow it. And that's the part that is so insidious. My parents were immersed in a system that gave them little opportunity to act any other way. It was embedded in the law. Although they believed in justice, and tried hard to raise us with notions of morality, they were ultimately prisoners of this society. I'm not trying to justify their inaction, but I do understand it. They were very conventional people. They did not have the sort of brave and courageous constitution that would enable them to fight the system. They simply closed their eyes to it, as most people do. I wish their sense of humanity had been able to overcome this stark reality. Others did. Even then I knew that this was possible. But I have never blamed them.

Everything about life in apartheid South Africa was a contradiction. Blacks were not to be trusted under any circumstances. Yet we trusted them with the most valuable of treasures: our lives. They raised our precious children; they made our food; they drove us around, polished our valuables, kept our homes sparkling and beautiful. And yet they were not to be trusted, in no way, not ever. The irony was insane, absurd. It was right in front of our eyes, and yet we couldn't really see it or feel it. Our whole world revolved around the colour black and the colour white, as if this was woven into the very fabric of existence. But, of course, while you are steeped in it, nothing is as visible as when you step out of it.

## CHAPTER 2

# SECOND MOTHER

Florrie came into my life when I was born; she had been employed specially to look after me. She was the second nanny in our household, because Margie and Pam had Elizabeth to look after them. Elizabeth was pretty cranky and crotchety. But I was lucky; I had Florrie.

Growing up, everyone I knew had nannies. You didn't have to be wealthy to have black maids and black workers and black quarters for your staff in your backyard. We grew up with nannies doing just about everything in our household. My sisters and I never made our beds, our school lunches; we never folded anything or pulled our clothes out of our own wardrobes. We never tidied up or cleaned up after ourselves. In South Africa, if you were white, this was the norm.

Our nannies came from faraway places that were mysterious to us. My sisters and I didn't know their surnames, we didn't know their history; we had no connection with their extended family. It's puzzling to consider living with someone, in your own house, and knowing so little about them. I remember asking my parents, 'Why does Florrie have a straw mattress and not a nice soft mattress like mine? Why does Florrie have no basin in her bathroom?' They simply answered, 'Because that is the way it is.' As a child, I certainly had a sense that my parents treated our workers better than some, but none of us treated them well. We never really thanked or acknowledged them. I am ashamed to say it, but we took them completely for granted.

In many households, the nannies amounted to a replica of the mistress of the home. My mum was a glorious cook, and she taught the nannies how to prepare her dishes. These black women made better matzo ball soup than my granny! My mother lived a white woman's life: she volunteered as president for the local community council, she played tennis, played bridge, saw friends for tea and kept herself busy. My mother did not really look after her children, our nannies did.

My mother was loving and warm, but she wasn't affectionate. She was too pragmatic for hugs. In fact, her cuddles were so few and far between that I remember begging her for them. But I got my fill of hugs from Florrie. I thought of her as 'my Florrie', and my mummy too, and she gave me lots of affection and love. I felt as though I was her baby. She loved me so much that she eventually named her own little baby girl Ronni. Somewhere out there in South Africa lives a 60-year-old black woman with a challenging name.

How I loved Florrie. It is only now, as I look back, that I realise how isolated Florrie must have been, away from her family and children. She looked after me while her village looked after her kids . . . wherever that village was. She would have had every reason in the world to be miserable or bitter. And yet she never appeared to be. She had this beautiful laugh and she gave me so much love and warmth. I can still smell her scent, feel her skin. She was beautiful, so soft and round, with twinkling eyes, and was always smiling with these big dimples. Maybe she was seventeen, or twenty. I don't really know, but she wouldn't have been much older than that. Just thinking of her, my eyes fill with tears.

And so, from birth, I was always with my Florrie and she was always with me. She carried me strapped to her back as she did the chores. I remember playing with her at the park, in our garden and around the house. I'd sit on the steps at the back of our house, which led to the black quarters where she lived, and eat her delicious food. The maids ate the cheap cuts of meat, but they'd cook it for hours, and it was so succulent and soft, and had the most delicious flavour. We'd eat it with mealiepap, maize flour porridge made into a ball, and you'd dip it into the meat and gravy. It was their food; it was not the food we ate at our family table. But I did eat it, sitting on her knee, in her arms, in my happy place.

One day, when I was about eight years old, Florrie didn't come and wake me up for school in the morning, as she always did. And she didn't make my breakfast, or my school lunch; my school uniform wasn't on the end of my bed waiting for me. She had gone. When I asked my mother, she said Florrie had had to go home. That is all I remember being told. And that was the end of life with Florrie as I knew it. To my parents, this disappearance wasn't greatly significant; it was simply a bit inconvenient. But I was devastated. I knew Florrie truly loved me, as I loved her, so her disappearance was bewildering. I felt abandoned and I internalised the heartache. But I had no one to share it with now that she had left without a trace. She was immediately replaced, of course, but by someone who could never fill her place.

This was not an uncommon scenario in apartheid South Africa. Nannies were often called back to their homes if something happened in their own families. To this day, I don't know what really happened to Florrie. I've always wanted to find her, to thank her, but I didn't even know her last name, and neither did anyone in our family. There was no trace of her except for her presence in my mind. I never really recovered from that loss. She was so important to me, though I don't know if she ever knew it; my beloved Florrie was the first person who showed me unconditional love.

These beautiful people came in and out of our childhood lives, and no adult thought it helpful to explain why. It was considered inconsequential, as if they were utterly expendable to us—except, of course, that they weren't. These relationships had depth and impact, they were a major part of our lives and their disappearance left scars. It is with great sadness that I retell a familiar story for white South Africans of my generation. We all lost love. This was a covert part of the tragedy of apartheid South Africa. Our scars, however, will never compare to the unspeakable traumas perpetuated against black South Africans. I have no words for the atrocities committed.

We had a gardener too. I never knew his name. I wish I had known.

# CHAPTER 3

# LEMONADE

It was rainy on the night my dad was late coming home from work. He was an architect, and he'd been driving back after visiting a synagogue that he had designed. But five o'clock came, and then six o'clock, so by the time the phone rang the air was tense. Margie was doing her homework and I was feeding my pet silkworms with mulberry leaves from our tree. I don't remember any other details. I do remember my mother picking up the phone and it being the police. The rest is a complete blur.

The next morning, I ran into my parent's bedroom as I often did, and I found the bed empty. My father was still not home. Neither was my mother. I jumped in nonetheless, and was under their sheets when my sisters joined me to tell me what was happening. My father had been in a terrible car accident, a head-on collision through no fault of his own, and had broken every bone in his body. He'd been completely smashed, from his bones to his internal organs. He was in such a critical condition that they didn't think he would live through the night.

But against all the odds, my father did make it through the night, and would make it through the next night, and the next. He held on, but there was no sense of how this would pan out. In time, the massive scale of his recovery became clear to us, and we all coped in different ways. Pam turned to her friends. (She was sixteen.) I turned to my mother. (I was six years old.) And Margie turned to God. As a very strong-willed eleven-year-old, Margie decided to make a pact with God. If our father survived, she would observe the Jewish traditions and rituals to the letter, and this would be no small feat. She asked none of us to believe with her, she just needed our support to make our household kosher, to go to synagogue every Saturday, and to help her observe the requirement of not using electricity on the Sabbath. This included not talking on the phone, which was a big deal for her. Margie was popular, and the landline was her lifeline. We all knew that our home phone was really *her* phone. On Saturdays, the phone rang off the hook; it was always for her and we had the chance to play secretary. Meanwhile she chose to hibernate in her Pat Boone–wallpapered cave reading a book, as it's forbidden to write on the Sabbath. I don't know how she (or we) survived! Regardless, we all honoured her pact and it had a huge impact on me, in terms of watching someone fulfil their conviction. She stuck to her commitment until she became an adult.

And whether Margie and God did their magic, or whether it wasn't his time, my dad came through the worst of it and survived. He needed to remain in hospital for two years, though we didn't know that at the time. All we knew was that, in an instant, life was never the same for any of us. We were a household of women now—my sisters, my mother and, of course, our maids.

My father had been successful as an architect, and loved playing golf and rugby and watching sport. He enjoyed classical music and playing bridge. But everything changed after that day. It was months before we, his girls, were even allowed to visit him in hospital. When we finally did, the first thing I remember seeing were his legs hanging up from ropes and his arms in plaster. I was completely terrified. His face was yellow and blue, he had cuts everywhere and he had no teeth. He told me to come sit on his bed, but I was too scared and refused. Somebody picked me up and sat me on the end of the bed. He was in there, somewhere; he just didn't look anything like my dad.

Many, many operations later, the doctors said my father would never walk again. His right leg could not be reconstructed to function. It was completely stiffened by the metal pins used to keep it together. His left leg was lame and could not hold the weight of his body. So he had to start to learn how to use his arms and hands. And while the physiotherapists and doctors treated him in hospital during those years, my mother had no husband or income to rely on, with three children to look after and a household staff who relied on her for their livelihood. In her own way, she would also have to learn to walk. She had to start working straight away to make a living, something she had never had to do since her married life began.

But boy, did she work after that accident! She didn't sit still for a minute. She needed to make money in the quickest way she knew how, so she threw herself into whatever was going to put food on our table. She sold wallpaper door-to-door, encyclopaedias door-to-door, and cooked for a school tuckshop on the side. She was such a practical person—totally no-nonsense. Everything she did was done without heaviness or complaint. And then she hit on something big. A friend asked if she would bake for his bowling club, and the orders started rolling in. It was the simplest way she could envisage—though in reality it wasn't simple—cakes, cakes and more cakes. In order to survive without my father's income, my mother became a cake baker from home. She would bake 250 cakes a week, with two mixmasters and one big oven. Our house forever smelt like vanilla essence.

One of my earliest memories is helping my mother pack the car full of cakes. My food delivery career began then, in a sense, way before my first OzHarvest van. We had this little car, and she'd had shelves built inside the boot. Layers of cakes would also adorn our seats. Sometimes I went kicking and screaming, but as I was the youngest I was the nominated *schlepper*. (That's the Yiddish word for a human mule!) I was quite the little helper and never dropped a cake. There were chocolate cakes, vanilla cakes, lemon cakes and coconut cakes—all of which I was allowed to help ice. My reward was licking the bowl, though I must say that incentive wore off after a while, given we were delivering 250 cakes a week. It's hard to believe she managed those numbers, but she did. Our little kitchen was a factory. My mother and the maids ran this little business like a well-oiled machine. And I can see now that she was absolutely entrepreneurial, although we didn't know the word back then. She took every opportunity up for grabs, as well as creating her own.

What is amazing is that I never remember seeing my mother in despair or suffering during that difficult time. I only remember her warmth, her smile, her beautiful energy and her unshakeable will, as she ran back and forth to the hospital, nurturing my dad, her business and us. Maybe there was a volcano of grief or anger waiting to erupt deep within her, but it never did. Not in front of us, at least. To us, she was Pollyanna, making the best of everything. Call it denial, call it what you will, but she quickly became a role model for us girls, one of strength and courage. She managed it all with grace and positivity, keeping us close to her side all the while.

My sisters and I thought our mother the most remarkable person we had ever met. I always credited my energy and my positivity to her. She had this resilient spirit of managing and coping and surviving. She turned around our challenging situation so fast. She fed us and clothed us and managed all the affairs herself, becoming this self-sufficient businesswoman, despite having been looked after her whole life, until then.

My father worked hard in hospital and learnt to use his hips to propel himself forward. He'd been given a caliper splint to hold up the lame leg, and the stiff leg could lean on a walking stick. We all watched him walk out of that hospital, upright. He was limping, clumsy, but walking. He'd made himself learn to walk again, in his way. We were watching a miracle unfold before our eyes—the miracle of his will. From that day on, he redesigned his life to compensate for his new body. Life had given him lemons, yet he found a way to make lemonade. He just got on with it, and I didn't realise that was exceptional. It didn't occur to me to think anything of it, until many years later.

Nothing in my parent's relationship seemed to change after the accident. They had always been—and continued to be—very romantic. They still walked down the street holding hands, like young lovers. And they always slept *lepeltjie*, which means spooning in Afrikaans. My dad continued to tell my mother she had the best legs on earth, and she maintained he was the most handsome man she'd ever known. The only change was that their hand-in-hand walk was at a slower pace than the one they used to take.

Believe it or not, it was only when I was 44 years old and giving the eulogy at my father's funeral that I realised, for the first time in my life, that he had been disabled. It had never even occurred to me. None of us had treated him that way, and I realised we never had because he had never thought of himself in that way. Everything he'd done and worked for had completely disappeared after the accident. But he had not had a jot of self-pity. He hadn't blamed anyone. He had simply carried on with his differently abled life, with no discussion of all he had lost.

That day, I sifted through my memories of him. I remembered how he'd modified his car so all his gears could be used by hand. (This was before automatic cars.) I remembered how his private practice had completely dissolved during his time in hospital, so he'd chosen to find a job working for someone else. I remembered how he'd taken up amateur photography and started painting as a hobby, and how happy they had made him. And I remembered how I'd come to building sites with him as a child, and he'd put down his walking stick and slowly, very slowly climb up on ladders to check building structures. It was terrifying to watch. But he was a stubborn, proud, immensely brave man.

It was true that my father was a victim of a serious accident. He could have stayed a victim. He could have not worked again for the rest of his life. He had every reason not to. He also could have been a misery to be around. But he chose not to limit himself. He made a deep choice about how he was going to live his life, and how he was going to deal with physical pain. He evolved. How had he really coped? What had gone through his mind? How had he dealt with the extreme pain he felt in his body for the rest of his life? I really don't know. He never spoke about it. He just continued on, living the best way he knew how. And he smiled a lot—not a smile that covered anything up, a smile that lit up the room. It took me a long time to recognise his part in my life, and his spirit, because I never thought to give him any credit for the part he played. He made it look so seamless that I took it for granted. But, consciously or not, he taught me to make the best of every situation that life presented me, even the unexpected ones. He taught me to look for the things that are life-giving, even in the face of loss. And within that, he taught me to be grateful for every moment I am alive, because no opportunity to be alive should be squandered.

My parents did not have the courage to fight the horrors of apartheid, but they were brave and courageous people nonetheless. They demonstrated their courage by living their lives with a strong will, acceptance and grace, even when those lives were dramatically rearranged. Their attitude served their lives, served each other, and served our family, and there is no doubt that I inherited many of their ways of being, by virtue of being their daughter. But really, recognising my father's life story at 44 years of age was a turning point. I realised I'd lived with a miracle before my eyes most of my life, I just hadn't known it. At that moment, I made a conscious decision to wake up every morning and choose my attitude towards my life, no matter what circumstances it was throwing my way.

CHAPTER 4

# TRAILBLAZER

My mother had made the best of her new role of homemaker and breadwinner, keeping our lives afloat and our family together. But it was through Selma Browde that I first saw a different side of what a woman could be.

While my parents were entertaining their friends, hosting bridge parties many nights a week—even after the accident—Selma was having evening parties of a very different kind. Her parties were sophisticated, intellectual and multi racial—despite the racist laws. Selma and her husband, Jules, were our next-door neighbours. They had sons who were roughly our ages and were at school with me and my sisters. And one of their sons, Alan—who was one year older than me—was also the love of my childhood life. But that is a story for later.

Selma was a doctor and Jules a successful, celebrated advocate and, later, a judge. They were dedicated to human rights, and were very well known, each in their own right, certainly within the Johannesburg intellectual circle. My parents thought the Browdes were amazing. They were outspoken anti-apartheid activists, while my parents absolutely weren't. My parents were clever, they were decent, they were salt of the earth, but they were not working to change South Africa.

For a long time during my childhood, Selma was at medical school, though in my mind she was always a doctor because she was always working. She officially became a doctor in 1959, and it was during her internship that she gave birth to her third son. She began working in a small hospital that, in those days, was called the 'Non-European Hospital', situated opposite the main whites-only Johannesburg Academic Hospital. She was a trailblazer medically. She was a trailblazer in so many ways. She was innovative. She pushed for palliative care in South Africa. She was ahead of her time in many aspects of her medical career but, more importantly, she always took action on her ideas. Her intellect worked to her advantage because she actually turned it into deeds.

But Selma was not only a progressive in her career as a radiation oncologist; she was also a politician, a health activist and an academic. She was the first city councillor for the Progressive Party, the liberal left wing of the all-white parliament. Selma was also the only woman on the Johannesburg City Council. She was responsible for sport and education programs for the disadvantaged. She was involved in so many aspects of black rights. People used her as their representative by coming directly to her home with their problems. She was completely focused on improving conditions for those who were politically disenfranchised.

Selma was smart, exotic and beautiful. She never chased publicity, but it chased her. She was statuesque, and she intimidated me at certain times in my childhood. She wore unusual clothes that I hadn't laid eyes on before, such as kimonos and kaftans, and even saris occasionally. I don't remember my mother getting dressed up in that sort of way. My mother was practical. She'd drive half an hour out of town to buy us the cheapest clothes at an Indian bazaar. We had our fill of glamour through Selma. She always had orange legs from the dodgy fake tans of the 1950s, and she had an expression of being deep in some very important thought, yet she could also focus on you intently. Sometimes that was terrifying.

My sisters and I were in and out of the Browde house all the time; in some ways, perhaps, we were the girls she never had, and her sons were the boys my father never had. In other ways, though, she was more like a big sister. My sister Margie was great with her hands. She was barely a teenager when she was offered the grand job of putting rollers in Selma's hair, teasing it, lacquering it and styling it. And though I was the little one, just wandering around smelling all her perfume and make-up, what I saw through Selma was that a woman could be anything she chose to be.

Viewed through my young eyes, Selma and Jules were the epitome of a power couple. And although there was indeed something powerful about them, they also had such humanity. They were warm. They were beloved friends of ours, essentially family. We were all so close and intertwined that they even made a hole in their fence so that we could share their swimming pool without having to ask. We definitely got kudos from our peers at school for being their neighbours. And yet, Selma was complex and was insecure on many levels. She felt guilty about everything. She was all about what she could have and should have done. Especially about having worked while her children were still very young. That sort of thing torments her to this day, as a 93-year-old woman.

I was in my late twenties when my mum became devastatingly ill. My mother was such a traditional person, she wasn't in awe of anybody. But she knew how to be a loyal friend. And it was during her challenging last days that I came to witness the depth of their friendship. I saw that what my mother and Selma had was a kind of shared devotion. And after my mother died, Selma and I became close friends. Our connection became deeper; we became two women, not a little girl and a lady. I don't ever recall thinking of her as a role model, but, undoubtedly, she would become one. Many years later, Selma would also be the vessel for one of the most powerful moments of my life. I just didn't know it then.

Looking back, what I have come to understand about Selma was that she was someone who could merge her career—and a passionate one at that—with moral commitment. The people around me worked to have a job so they could live. But Selma chose to work in the areas she cared about in her life. She chose to make a difference. She was unusual. We didn't know anyone else quite like that. She was making such a deep, subtle impression on me. I feel privileged that I got to witness someone throughout my childhood who had the courage to make a stand for what she believed in. And a woman at that.

CHAPTER 5

# LOST DIAMOND

One day, when I was three years old, my mother found a grubby ring jumbled among my toys. Despite the concealed sparkle, it didn't seem like a ring from a cereal box! She sensed it might be valuable. Suspicious about how I'd acquired it, she went and asked Selma. Of course, it was Selma's! It was in fact a very valuable diamond ring that she hadn't known was missing. Selma hadn't realised what she'd lost, my mother had hardly realised what she'd found and I had no idea what I'd been given. Selma in her wisdom went and asked her cheeky boy Alan about it, and he, at the tender age of four, responded, 'Mummy, you told me that this ring was going to be for the girl I'm going to marry, so I gave it to Ronni!' It was the cutest thing. I was betrothed before I could even speak in full sentences. I was well on my way to becoming a child bride!

Every single day of my life, growing up in South Africa, I'd hang out with my husband-to-be, Alan. I can't tell you how much I adored him. I loved everything about him, and playing in the garden with him when we were little kids was the best thing in my life. We'd play. He'd tease me. He'd torment and taunt me. But I continued to be absolutely and utterly in love with him, even though sometimes he was just horrible. And when he wasn't being horrible to me, well, that was pure magic.

Alan was a born leader. Throughout our growing-up years, he was very popular, and a force to be reckoned with. By the time we were teenagers, his feet were so huge that his shoes had to be imported from America! He would walk me to all my weekend activities. He was my assigned protector. But it was also his personality that was big and playful. There were no rules with Alan. He was a total free spirit, with a sharp temper. People just did anything he said. Once, as a teenager, he picked up a police officer by the collar because he was arresting a black woman on the sidewalk. He didn't know his own strength. He was also courageous, the kind of person who always did the right thing at the right time. He was the son of Selma and Jules, after all, so human rights were a part of his DNA.

You would hear Alan long before you saw him. His booming voice gave me comfort, and I felt safe with him around. He had the best smile, with these big gaps in his teeth. He was an incredible sportsman, totally charismatic and spontaneous, and everybody followed him and loved him. But I loved him in a different way. It wasn't a romantic love, I just wanted anything for him that he wanted. I never asked for anything from him, and never imagined I was worthy of him in a romantic way. It was just the deepest love I had ever felt for a boy. I thought, *This must be what it feels like to have a brother*. I guess, to me, he was my brother. Sometimes I was his confidante. Mostly, I was the person he could bully, and that was enough. Because I felt I knew who he was deep down. I knew how lovable he truly was, and I felt he loved me in his own way. I didn't rely on him, but if I needed him, he'd be there. He always came first though. It had to suit him. I knew and accepted that.

Every afternoon, when the home bell rang, we'd walk right through the school campus, which was miles and miles, and he'd say, 'Little Ronni Hellmann, carry my bags.' And I'd run over and carry all his things, all his books and bags and cricket bats—the lot. I never questioned it. It never for a second occurred to me to say, 'Hey, come on . . . No!' He was my best friend and I worshipped him. I'd walk the longest way, toppling over from the weight of all his stuff, while he walked ahead of me with his friends, laughing and having a great time—hands free!

Oh, the poor little schmozzle that was me. Carrying all that cricket gear for a bit of love. Not a shred of self-worth to be seen. In hindsight, it's no surprise that my relationship with my cousin Michelle was more than a little fraught. Michelle was six months older than me and she was beautiful and perfect in every way. She was smart at school and she was also a dancer. Without being fully aware of it, I believe our parents created a strange, competitive edge between us. When I was six years old, I asked to go to dance lessons, just like Michelle. Well, I only had one dance lesson, because the teacher said I was pretty bad and my mother said, 'No way, you are not going to any more dance lessons. We can't afford to invest in two left feet!' So by the time I was six, I already believed I was a terrible dancer, and to this day I still believe that.

Michelle, however, was special. Special to me meant that you were smart at school and popular, and that people wanted to be around you. No one wanted that from me. I was never one of the popular girls. And

I was not pretty. No one told me to my face that I was ugly. But no one told me I was pretty either, ever. My sister Pam was the beautiful one, and my sister Margie had all the personality. So in my eyes, I was the *nebbish*. In Yiddish, that means, the poor, unfortunate soul.

Compared to Michelle, I didn't measure up. The only thing I had going for me was that I was really good at sport, and she wasn't. But even though I excelled, she was still more valued as a team member. No one would ever dare leave her out! She had this sort of know-how of a beautiful and accomplished person. She was my absolute nemesis and often I would cry myself to sleep thinking about it all. I'm certain she had no idea, and years later we became real friends. But the whole Michelle situation had an incredible power over me at that time. She had all the boys after her at high school, and had one boyfriend after another, and she had all the girlfriends; it was totally traumatic. She graduated from school with great results while I was terrified I wouldn't even pass. But I managed. I was not academic, but I passed. I never considered for a moment that I could do anything significant in my life, nor did I have the ambition.

Just before the end of high school, though, my boyfriend drought lifted and I met Des at our Jewish youth group. Des was four years older than me and was at university. An older man! I'm sure it gave me an edge among my friends. He was smart, and if I read a book, he'd say, 'What did you think of that book?' And I'd say, 'Well, what did *you* think of the book?' Then I'd make sure I thought the same thing. I had no capacity whatsoever to value my own intellect. I didn't feel any of my opinions were worthy of expression.

My parents really liked Des, and my mother thought he was a wonderful catch because his father was a lawyer. 'He'll do. I don't think you'll find someone better,' she once said to me. And when I finally graduated from high school, I desperately wanted to go to art school or to study architecture. But my parents said, 'You can't, you don't have that kind of talent.'

So, you see, although my parents displayed such quiet positivity and courage in their daily life, in many ways they lived with an overall sense of limitation. It took me years to realise that. My mother believed in settling for what you had. Feelings were irrelevant. She was absolutely pragmatic. And she was a compromiser. I followed her example and said yes to things because I felt limited. Both my parents' limitations were internalised and expressed through me.

For a very long time in my life, I believed in those limitations. And I'm not saying there wasn't a good reason for them. My mother had to help us all survive after my father's life-changing accident, and my father had lost so much. It followed that self-respect and dance classes, artistry and being in love—these were inconsequential to survival. We were taught to consider things sensibly and rationally. There was no room for trying or choosing. There was only room for getting on with it. The name of the game was to make sure you weren't left without. It was a silent sense of limitation and scarcity, but silent undercurrents within families are often much stronger than waves.

This idea of scarcity existed not just about things like money, it extended to me as a human being. I received the message that there was a shortage of talent, beauty, boyfriends and options, and I internalised that message on some level. There was no room for trying my hand at following artistic fantasies when we lived in such insufficiency. Of course Alan could treat me so badly. I had little to no sense of self-worth. Perhaps it's no accident that my life's work is about scarcity, abundance and redistribution. It's about asking, 'Who has extra to give? Who doesn't have enough?' Discovering abundance through my work led me to learn—really learn—that the world had so much to offer. That I had so much to offer. The energy spent on what other people have is energy that could be much better spent. It has become a beautiful exchange. I learnt that I had a lot of energy, and that I could lead and love and know my feelings and my mind. I learnt that I have unique talents and have witnessed the unique talents of so many people around me. The abundance is everywhere. But it's a funny thing with abundance, because it only appears when you choose to see it.

Sometimes I think about that diamond ring buried in my toys. How could we have known the value hidden beneath its dulled brilliance?

CHAPTER 6

# THE PLACE I CALLED HOME

My first experience of knowing something was wrong with South African society was at the Jewish youth movement that I attended from the age of six. My parents would drive my sisters and me to Habonim every Sunday, happy to be rid of us for a few hours. It was essentially a youth group for Jewish kids, to explore their Jewish identity. I went there every week, and it was the safest place to talk about the fact that South Africa wasn't okay.

Habonim was never frivolous. It was socialising without any drinking or parties, but with camaraderie and community. We would meet and have discussions about how to have a meaningful life, and about mending the world by behaving constructively in every way that is beneficial to humans. It was the first time I heard the concept of *tikkun olam*. Our leaders at Habonim talked about *tikkun olam* all the time. Translated from Hebrew, it literally means 'to repair (*tikkun*) the world (*olam*)'. And the way it was explained was that it is incumbent upon every person to repair the world, to do our part when we see an injustice. It came to be used as an umbrella term, exclusively to describe acts of social justice. You can imagine what an ironic, difficult idea this was from a practical point of view if you were growing up in apartheid South Africa. My only real-life reference point for *tikkun olam* was the work of Selma and Jules. The majority of us didn't dare to face the ramifications of doing *anything* in the face of injustice! Apart from getting arrested, how any of us could put into practice this crucial notion was beyond me. Nonetheless, it was an idea that stuck with me for life, and would feature strongly in later years.

Most of my values came from Habonim, without a doubt, as my parents didn't express their values in words. At Habonim everything was spoken about, everyone was outspoken, and our leaders were the kind of people we all wanted to be. Though teenagers themselves, they were on the front lines, demonstrating, actively living their beliefs. They helped us shape our liberal views, of equality and socialism, and this was deeply meaningful to me. The newly established state of Israel was also a core element of the Habonim agenda. It was idealistic, but it represented more than an abstract 'pioneering spirit of Israel' point of view; it was about the lives of actual pioneers in Israel, and about the lives of individuals who were making a difference in the world. These stories brought our values to life.

From an historical point of view, as Jews, we had only just survived Hitler's massacre, many without all our family members intact. By the age of fifteen, I knew that Jews now (supposedly) had freedom. And with the state of Israel, we (supposedly) had a homeland too. Yet everywhere we looked in South Africa, there was no freedom, there was only a system of bullying and fear and cruelty—a privileged minority dominating a repressed majority. Even a child could see that none of us was free. We were all part of a rigid, authoritarian system that said we had to bear in mind the colour of our skin whatever we did and wherever we went. Guilt and shame—however unconscious—were part of our existence. This was troubling to all of us. And yet, as part of the white population, we were safe within this devastatingly racist system. The system was not of our creation, but simply by being white and living in South Africa—if we didn't fight against it—we perpetuated it. If we just stayed out of trouble and behaved, ignoring what we knew about social justice, life would be pretty fine. But the toll of this denial was always there, in the back of our minds, and it led to a bipolar existence, to say the least.

As a school kid, you couldn't really be an activist, at least that was my understanding. Those opportunities seemed to happen at university. Then you could join things. You could become an active anti-apartheid fighter if you wanted to, though this would put you at a degree of risk and danger, and most probably gaol. You had to be brave to do that. Really brave. The closest I came to being politically involved was living next door to Selma and Jules while they were involved in human rights work. In the meantime, Habonim educated us about the problems in our country, but we couldn't take part in expressing any of those views outside our little circle.

When I was seventeen, I graduated from high school, and my parents decided it was best for me to go to university in Israel. There was a scholarship program that paid for Jewish kids to go to university there, with all living expenses covered. I think my parents found the idea very attractive because it removed all financial pressure to provide for me. It was decided that I should study Art History and English Literature at the Hebrew University of Jerusalem, so they packed me up, and off I went. I was very nervous about the idea. I had struggled a lot at school camps, just by being away from home. I'd cry myself to sleep at night. I was always homesick. I didn't even sleep well at friends' places. I wasn't a big, brave, independent human being; I was still very much a child. Thinking back, I'm not sure how my parents just went ahead and made that decision for me. We were so close and interconnected, but they just completely let me go. At the time, I didn't think I could live a single day without my mother. I'd never been out of South Africa; I'd never even been on a plane. I have no idea how I boarded that flight. But I did it. I got on that plane and I left, just like that, though I cried all the way. I left behind my boyfriend, Des, too, although I knew he had plans to come to Israel a year later. At that time there was no way of knowing how things would work out between us. The only saving grace was that my sister Margie and her new husband Eli had moved to Israel six months earlier, though we wouldn't be in the same city. Still, it was family.

So I left that confusing country of my birth, as consciously as one could as a teenager, which is to say not very consciously at all. I just took one little suitcase. It never occurred to me to prepare for not living in South Africa again. But at the end of my first year of university in Israel, Des arrived, so it was obvious I would stay longer. Little did I know I would never again return to South Africa, at least not as a place I called home.

# CHAPTER 7

# MANDELA

Jules Browde, Selma's husband, used to tell us this story about when he was a young law student at Witwatersrand University, in South Africa in the 1940s. The year was 1946, and the apartheid government was still two years away from coming to power. Although black students were not allowed to live in the university's residences, or use the sport facilities, a limited number were still permitted to study there. This particular day was the first day of class, and the all-white cohort of students was assembling in the law library for a lecture. The lecture was just about to begin when a tall young black student entered and looked around for a place to sit. He noticed an empty seat next to Jules and walked towards it. As soon as it was obvious where he was going to sit, the student on the other side of the empty chair made a great show of getting up and going to sit on the far side of the table. He was making a clear statement: he wouldn't sit next to a black man. Quietly mortified, Jules, without saying anything, indicated his welcome for the man to sit beside him. At the end of the lecture, Jules introduced himself to the young student and they shook hands. That day was the beginning of a friendship that lasted for the rest of their lives. The student's name was Nelson Mandela.

People often ask me who are the leaders I admire, and this story always comes to mind. I was always blown away by it, because it represents a tiny portal into the kind of daily degradation that this person—this man—had to rise above every single day of his life just to exist. This story was just one tiny awful incident among so many he would be likely to face each day, each week, throughout his life. What does it take for a person to transcend continual personal insult? What does it take to transcend racism, oppression, exploitation, bloodcurdling corruption? It may not be easy to relate to this scenario; I can barely contemplate it myself. But just imagine, everywhere you go—every supermarket you enter, every bus you catch, every train you ride, every job you apply for—people are excluding you, tormenting you, degrading you and your family in every possible way. What would that do to you? What would that do to your spirit? What does it do to your humanity?

Mandela went to prison prepared to die for a cause, prepared to blow himself up if that is what it would take to bring down apartheid. He was sentenced to life imprisonment, did hard labour for eighteen of those years, suffered brutality, physical torment and blatant cruelty. He had every right in the world to apportion blame, to feel rage. His people had suffered atrocities for centuries, atrocities that deemed them non-human, less than animals. And a whole country, whole societies, had insidiously followed suit.

But the astonishing reality is that when Mandela walked out of prison 27 years later, he shook hands with the very people who had put him there. And then he convinced them to break down the walls of apartheid. He transformed a whole society: persuaded them to accept him, to change their beliefs about him, to the point that he was not only welcomed back but was made their leader. He rose above mortal ideas of justice. He moved past insults, abuse and blame, in a way that was godlike. Because he did it with absolute compassion. And that compassion tore through what had seemed impenetrable. It's hard to understand how he did this. But he did.

How does a human being move beyond anger, blame, excuses, trauma, insane levels of injustice? How do we stop blaming the government, the institutions, the systems, the supermarkets, the fossil fuel companies, the meat eaters, our boss, our parents? Something happened to Mandela in those 27 years. Something deep and life-giving. Mandela had an inner transformation, one that gave him one task in the world and one task only. And that was to embrace his perpetrators in order to assemble a just society of respect and integrity. Somehow, he won a battle within himself, so that he was no longer willing to blow up a system to bring about freedom, and no longer needed to resort to justifiable violence. He had been willing to die for what he believed in. And he did die in that prison. Not in the way we know death, but in the sense that the part of him that had a million reasons to be angry died. The terrorist within him died. Even the freedom fighter within him died. Because there was nothing left to 'fight'. He died and won the greatest battle within himself. He won his inner freedom. He restored his humanity. In doing so, he changed the world. This is why he was a great leader. This is why I look up to him.

Decades later, in 1990, my family and I would huddle around a TV to watch Mandela walk out of gaol. My husband and I had waited for this moment since we were teenagers, now I was almost a 40-year-old woman. It seemed impossible that this was happening, yet it was just as I had always imagined it. He walked out, smiling, gracious, dignified. He was the man the world had been waiting to see, and not only because he was the legendary Nelson Mandela, but because he was the potential of the human in all of us.

# PART 2

# ISRAEL

# CHAPTER 8

# LAND OF HUMMUS AND FALAFEL

Even though I'd spent most of my life hearing about our 'homeland', Israel did not feel like home right away. It was exhilarating in many ways, but also foreign as anything. Every aspect of my life in Israel was different from what I had known. I had to adapt to so much. I had to learn Hebrew—I only knew the basics from school—and during my first month I virtually died of starvation. I'd never eaten a tomato. I'd never eaten an olive, a cucumber, a zucchini, a radish or a salad. I'd never eaten hummus or falafel or cream cheese, and I hated boiled eggs. My South African diet had exclusively consisted of hot chocolate and peanut butter toast for breakfast, and chips and lamb chops for dinner. That was it. After eating nothing but bread for my first month in Israel, I was hungry; hungry enough to force myself to taste these strange new foods. I had to learn how to eat in Israel, and quickly, because there wouldn't be a lamb chop or a chip in sight for the next twenty years! It turned out to be pretty exciting, actually, and I didn't miss home at all. I missed my parents. But not home. I couldn't find much to miss about South Africa.

There was a whole bunch of us from our South African Habonim group at my university. Initially I lived on campus, but it was so soulless that eventually I moved into an apartment with a friend. We had each other, but I still felt completely on my own. I'd never experienced anything like it. For starters, I'd always had a maid. None of the white South Africans I knew had ever *not* had a maid. I didn't even know how to do the most basic things, but I now had to stand on my own two feet. My first week I thought to myself, *This whole making your own bed thing is quite a lot of effort*. But very quickly looking after myself became an adventure. I could choose what to do, make my own decisions. I didn't know how to cook even one dish, so I would write letters to my mother, asking how do you make this? How do you make that? How do you roast potatoes? Then I'd wait patiently for her airmail replies. My mum had learnt to cook from her mother, but nothing had been passed on to me.

Jerusalem was fascinating. Just walking through the streets filled me with absolute awe. There was so much ancient history. South Africa had none of that. Here, just walking to my local bus stop I couldn't avoid following Jesus's footsteps—quite literally! History and religion were at my very fingertips. Basic errands were breathtaking. I'd follow my nose to hidden bakeries in tiny medieval-looking corners of quarry-stoned buildings just to get my hands on a baked pretzel.

During this time, Des was still my boyfriend, and we were doing the whole 'long-distance relationship' thing while he continued university in South Africa. I had waited for him patiently, and a little resentfully, but I was very well behaved. When he finally arrived, he and his Habonim friends had discussed lots of options for living arrangements, and they had decided that their hearts were absolutely set on living on a kibbutz.

A kibbutz is a collective community based on utopian ideas of socialism and communal living. In the early days of Israel, the kibbutz movement had its roots in agriculture: working the land and supporting the construction of the country. Imagine what socialism meant to white South Africans, who had come from a country where gross inequality, brutal injustice and unfair distribution of resources was the law and the norm. This was a chance to experience and engage in the exact opposite. This was a paradise of equality! A kibbutz was a complete contrast to the society they came from and they embraced it with fervour. It was also an opportunity for individuals from all walks of life to live on a farm, to do good for the country and to support its growth. They could finally take a stand openly, freely and by choice. It seemed like the ultimate way to live a value-driven Jewish life.

I had been happily enjoying Jerusalem and Israeli city life in general. I had not even considered a kibbutz lifestyle. In principle it seemed like a nice idea, but it was hard to imagine actually living there. I felt too young to make such a big decision, so I did what came naturally to me—I followed Des. I stumbled into kibbutz living like a dazed teenager, in exactly the same way that I had stumbled onto that plane from South Africa to Israel, thinking I would be gone for a year. The same way that I had stumbled into university to do the degree my parents decided I should do. My parents were thrilled by the decision to move to a kibbutz. It was a safe place and it provided financial security.

Life started to take a new shape and things gradually evolved. Those who were university educated went to a kibbutz not to use their degrees, but to kindle their pioneering spirit. I continued my degree and graduated while living on the kibbutz, over the next two years. But Des gave up studying law to be a pioneer, to work the land, and to philosophise his life away. He seemed liberated in some way, excited. I, on the other hand, had wanted to be an artist. I was studying art history at university, but it was just theory. I wanted to paint; I wanted to draw; I wanted to create pottery; I wanted to make art. However, I had literally nothing to show for this desire. I didn't have a portfolio, I didn't have any artwork of my own, I didn't have anything. I just had a feeling that this was my path. In a nutshell, as I really had no idea where I was headed, a kibbutz felt like as good an idea as any.

Socialism, in the way we experienced it on a kibbutz, was a society in which people chose to come together to work according to their ability, and receive according to an equal distribution system. The overarching idea was that if it was good for the society as a whole, it was good for the individual. Everything had to apply equally, which was the exact opposite to life in South Africa. For example, there was a time when Des and I brought back a little TV set from a trip we'd made. It was the only TV set on the kibbutz, and it had to go under serious tribunal assessment to decide if we could keep it. Finally, the decision was made that it could stay, as long as it was housed in the common room so everyone could enjoy it. Every decision had to consider the greater good. There was something quite magical about that mindset.

As a community, we were completely provided for and we were all treated equally. Money never changed hands there because there wasn't money as such. It didn't exist. We had coupons instead, which looked much like a perforated bingo card, that we could use at the one local kibbutz store in exchange for luxury items, such as chocolate and lollies and ice-cream. All our core basic needs were provided for, such as soap, coffee, tea, and cheap cigarettes if you smoked. Medication was free, from the kibbutz pharmacy, and a doctor and a nurse lived on the grounds. If we wanted to go out for the day, there was a communal kibbutz car that we were allowed to use three times a year. It had to be booked well in advance though, and the tension about whether it would be in working order was immense. These were our very real kibbutz problems.

We were 300 or so families coming together, with a whole range of agendas and reasons for ending up on a kibbutz. We lived in our little modular flats with tiny toy kitchenettes, because all meals were provided in the communal dining room. There was no real need for much else. However, many of us loved to bake at home. So first we lobbied for a mini stove-and-oven combo, then we asked for better kettles, and then we wanted bigger (small) fridges. We'd create miracles from these appliances in our little kitchenettes! We were always striving to make our homes just a bit homier. We also supported one another, like a very big family, and this was one of the many aspects of kibbutz life that was fantastic. My friends and I had beautiful, fun times together. We'd go for walks and nature was all around us. It was a special time and place. Finally, I was living in a community where we were all equal—at least within our walls.

Actually, there was one way in which inequality became visible on the kibbutz. Although our houses were structurally exactly the same, we had to furnish them ourselves. So if you had parents with money, you had more, and you had beautiful things. That was the only time inequality became visible, but it didn't seem to worry anyone. The principle was still that everything was essentially the same, and was communal. We all worked hard to do things for each other. There was a roster system for everything, and we worked six days a week, in the cause of the greater good. We believed as a whole that this was an idea worth spreading, one that could really work for the world. The only problem was . . . it didn't take long before I was secretly quite unsure about whether it was, in fact, working for me.

Having no particular qualification that was useful to the kibbutz, as a woman I was expected to work in the kids' house. From six weeks of age, children spent eight hours a day in a communal house. As you can imagine, there was so much to do. I was immediately put to work as a teacher's aide, for kids of twelve years and above. The kids seemed to love their lives on the kibbutz. They were free and wild, climbing trees and picking fruit. But as a 20-year-old, I really couldn't stand my job. I found the kids rude and the role lacking in fulfilment. I was folding their clothes, cleaning their rooms, providing their meals. It was a total drag. It wasn't that I knew exactly what I wanted to do for a job, but I certainly knew I didn't want to do this work. It was so depressing, but it didn't occur to me to be depressed. I became impatient instead.

Maybe it's my impatience that has often spurred me into action. I'm not so comfortable with uncomfortable feelings. I never know how to just feel them. Instead, they inspire action. And I wanted out of that drudgery. To escape my uncomfortable feelings I started daydreaming about buying stuff—outfits, fashion. Not the ideal preoccupation for a new socialist! I knew this consumer side of me would not be fulfilled on a kibbutz—that was impossible. So I started saving my kibbutz coupons, cashing them in like pocket money, then venturing off to the big smoke—Tel Aviv—to buy my own clothes.

There was a tailor on our kibbutz, my dear friend Stella, who had been a dress designer by trade. After years of working in the laundry, she was given the opportunity of creating a little shop for all of us, and making our clothes. I was into other fashion at that point, though. I wanted Indian fabrics; I wanted hippie stuff, I wanted to express myself somehow through my clothes. I had to do something with my artistic leanings! There seemed so little opportunity on a kibbutz to make my own choices, and fashion felt like a thrilling way to put my personal stamp on something. I wanted to feel like I had my own identity. Then one day, on one of my city fashion sprees, I had the bright idea of buying more than I needed and reselling them to other women on the kibbutz, those who wanted an individual identity too. If someone wanted exotic fabrics with bohemian designs, I was your woman. The small profit I made gave me extra cash to buy more beautiful clothes for myself. It worked well. I became the competition to the little kibbutz boutique. Even Stella started buying clothes from me. That was my first entrepreneurial attempt. I liked it and I wanted to do it more.

Meanwhile, Des was completely fulfilled. He loved life on the kibbutz. He worked in the fields, with tractors and combine harvesters—boys' toys. Maybe one or two of the women who worked in the orchard sometimes used a tractor, but when you were new, and a woman, you couldn't do that kind of thing. We hadn't earned the right yet. It's not like I was dying to jump on a tractor—I wasn't—but women were definitely limited, workwise. We were placed in service positions and traditional female roles. We didn't have a chance to live out the pioneer fantasy; we didn't have the opportunity to connect with the land.

The boys toiled for us. The land was tilled to supply the needs of the community. We grew cotton and sold cotton. We grew watermelons and sold watermelons. We had an orange orchard and sold oranges. Looking back, the men were generally happier than the women. They really lived out that pioneering fantasy, with their sweat and dirt-stained fingers. It was a satisfying romantic, pastoral life. But if a couple decided to leave the kibbutz, in general, you could bet your bottom dollar that it was the woman who had finally put her foot down and said, 'Enough! I'm outta here.' So out they went.

I felt just like those women, which was totally different from how Des felt. I felt lonely, somewhere deep within myself, but I didn't talk to my friends about my unfulfilled days. It didn't feel right to express my dissatisfaction. When everyone was working to find their place in one way or another the last thing anyone needed was a voice of dissent. The only person I could open up to was Des, and he was happy, and was sure that pretty soon I'd make it work too. He felt I'd adjust, it would simply take me time. It seemed so cool to be an idealist. I felt shame that maybe I wasn't one, and that I wasn't acclimatising fast enough. I just ploughed on, as I had been taught to do.

The dilemma of the kibbutz was that it brought up lifestyle questions every day, even if they were hidden in very secret parts of your heart and mind. Even though kibbutz life was a reality we had all chosen, the question was always there, *Is this working for me?* When you have made a choice to live an alternative lifestyle, you also know there is always something else to fall back on, to go back to. And that was me. I questioned, every single day. It was an abstract, secret torment.

Despite these reservations, I did have wonderful friends on the kibbutz, and many of these friendships continue to this day. I even had family—my sister-in-law and closest friend, Jenny (Des's sister), who joined us not long after we moved there. And when she married our gorgeous blue-eyed friend Neil, we lived in adjacent townhouses, with a common wall between us. Jenny and I used to talk to each other through the electricity socket. I'd wake up to her voice through the wall, 'Ronni, ARE YOU UP YET?' It was communal living to the nth degree. That was fun.

And then there was Neil. If anybody could make me feel that we were living in a funny kind of utopia, it was him. He loved the kibbutz so much, he was so social, and he was a total *chevreman*—Yiddish for a really jolly guy. He could mimic just about anybody, and we would roll around laughing. He always brought humour to a situation, and was so positive about the future in Israel. I can almost hear him now, 'See ya round like a bagel!' That's what he always said when we parted ways. I'm not even sure I knew what a bagel was at that time, but it always made me laugh.

Now and then, I'd have my romantic kibbutz moment. Every six weeks, we were rostered on to a special job. Mine was working with the calves in the cow shed. We had a dairy farm, and these babies needed to be fed and their pens needed to be cleaned. I absolutely loved that job. Even though this chore wasn't so different from those in the kids' house, it was when I was alone and in my overalls and dirty gumboots that I felt connected to the land. I felt truly connected to something bigger and greater than myself. It was a beautiful service in my eyes. I loved shovelling their manure; I loved making their world clean and comfortable. It was a strange kind of meditation for me, and I'd completely forget my usual mixed emotions. Unfortunately, this job wasn't available to me full time. But I longed for that one day to come around again and again. Me and the cows. It felt almost transcendent to nurture in this way.

# CHAPTER 9

# ISRAEL ATTACATO

In the summer of 1971, Des joined the army, which was and still is a compulsory part of being a citizen in Israel. Women didn't have to enlist then as they do now. I flirted with the idea of joining the army for all of three minutes before deciding I wasn't cut out for it. Not long after conscription, our friend Ian asked Diana to marry him, and our friend Paul asked Shirley, and so Des proposed to me. Well actually, it wasn't really a proposal. One day Des came home and said, 'They're all getting married because we'll get more army leave if we do, so . . . shall we get married too?' Everyone was doing it, so, as usual, I was like, 'Yep, sure, let's do this.'

We planned the timing of our wedding to suit our parents. They hadn't visited us before, hadn't seen our lives on the kibbutz, so it was a big deal. Within six months, the whole thing was organised and ready to go. There wasn't really much preparation at our end. The only choice we had was who to invite. The rest was sorted. After all, it was a kibbutz wedding with a kibbutz rabbi and kibbutz food. There were no real choices. You just put things in motion and they happened. My wedding dress arrived in the loving hands of my dearest aunt two days before the ceremony. She had painstakingly crocheted a white woollen wedding dress. I love that she made it for me, I really do. Every stitch was crocheted with love, but it was not designed with my body in mind! I absolutely hated how it looked on me. I just didn't have the heart or the guts to speak up about it. So I wore it. But I had a miserable wedding day because that dress clung to my bum and my hips and all my bumps, and I never wore clothes that did that. Where were Spanx when I needed them? I felt so uncomfortable and self-conscious—it was a mortifying experience to have on your wedding day! When I think about that day, it's the thing I remember the most—the sense of personal discomfort. In our wedding pictures, I look far from joyous. Granted, everyone pulled those long faces in the 1970s, but I was not a radiant bride! I was all of twenty years old.

We treated ourselves to a two-day honeymoon at the seaside resort of Nahariya—a popular holiday town known then for its terrible (but affordable) hotels, as well as for being the cradle of the Israeli mafia. Along with our luggage, we were accompanied by an in-law entourage. Des's family didn't think it was fair for us to go away without them. As you can imagine, it was incredibly romantic—me, my new husband, my in-laws, my sister-in-law and my cheeky brother-in-law!

Two years later Des redeemed himself from that absurd *hamula* honeymoon—*hamula* is Arabic slang for extended family/tribe—by organising a European getaway to celebrate him finishing his army term and my graduation from university. We had only just arrived in Italy when we saw a disturbing headline at a newspaper stand, on a glorious Roman morning: 'Israel Attacato'. We weren't a hundred per cent sure what it meant, but it did not sound good. We raced to buy an English-language newspaper, only to discover that war had broken out between Egypt, Syria and Israel. This was later known in Israel as the Yom Kippur war, because the surprise assault took place on the holiest day of the Jewish calendar. While everyone fasted and prayed on that sacred day, a barrage of bombs, jets and rocket launchers was unleashed.

I couldn't have been more relieved that we were in Europe, safe from all the mess. I absolutely did not want Des running off to war. But Des said, 'Ronni, we're going back.' It was a matter of honour for him. There was no way he would not join his peers. In reality, neither of us could have lived with ourselves if we hadn't returned. We rushed to the airport, but all commercial flights had been halted. We hung around the airport with a bunch of other determined Israelis, in the hope of finding a way back. And we did. We shoved and pushed our way onto a plane that was heading to Tel Aviv to repatriate stranded Italians and remove them from a war-torn country. It was a total fluke that we got on. It felt like a strange dream, a terrifying and absurd one at that.

We arrived at night, on the third or fourth day of the war, to a country under siege. I don't even know how the plane landed, as Israel was fully blacked out for self-defence. But miraculously, we did land. There were only a few cabs on the streets, all driven by the wives of husbands at war. We found a lady who would drive us at extortionist rates, but we were prepared to take any ride we could. The city had the strangest vibe I've ever felt in my life. I was terrified. Then, before I knew it, Des went straight to army camp. I barely had a chance to say goodbye in the rush and tumble of it all. I couldn't really even absorb that he was going to war, that he could die.

*Things will be fine*, I thought to myself. Israel's previous war had lasted six days so; believe it or not, it didn't occur to me to worry, or to consider that absolutely anything could happen: that this was war, real war. In hindsight, my thinking was ridiculous, but it was my first war. We were all new immigrants. What did we know about any of this? We were kids.

Everything changed on the kibbutz during that blurry time. Most of the men were gone, so women were fulfilling all the roles. Every day we lived with the roar of MiG jets soaring over the front line, and tanks clamouring across our main road. Air-raid sirens went off a few times a day and we'd run to fortified underground shelters to hide. I had to leave the kids' house indefinitely, to answer phones in the kibbutz office and sort the mail. Messages were coming in thick and fast about both people and situations. Though the war itself lasted about two and a half weeks, I didn't realise that a war doesn't officially end when the fighting ends. A war can drag on for months, due to the aftermath of injury and prisoners of war. I was living on my own in our little apartment, listening to all this crazy news every day when I found out that I was pregnant. A honeymoon baby. I couldn't believe it. I told no one. It wasn't the time to be sharing that sort of news. There wasn't time to think about such things.

There was an intricate messaging system relating to the war in those pre-internet days—someone saw so-and-so, and then someone else saw so-and-so, and that kept going; that's how we found out what was happening. It was a sort of grapevine. If you were a soldier passing another soldier, you'd say, 'If you see so-and-so, tell them to call my mother in Tel Aviv,' or wherever. And then you'd run to give the message to so-and-so who could then call the mother, the wife, the daughter—whoever it was. And it took a little while, but eventually I got word that Des was safe. We were getting all sorts of messages from soldiers—I'm okay, I'm okay, I'm okay. There were only three of our kibbutz soldiers we hadn't heard from: Shaul, one of our best friends Dudi, and our brother-in-law, Neil. Jenny had received four postcards from Neil very early on, but she hadn't heard from him since. We started getting worried, but we didn't let ourselves suspect the worst. We all supported each other, and we held onto hope. We were all in it together, and surely it was going to be okay. But the weeks passed and nothing was coming through for Jenny, or for Sandy, Dudi's girlfriend. They were worried sick. We all were. Every day I would sort through the mail, praying something would come, but it didn't. We were convinced that their messages were getting lost in the jumble of the chaotic aftermath of this devastating war. How could we ever consider that they could get hurt?

The weeks came and went and the silence became ominous. Messages had come from everyone else. Jenny was dropping kilos, seemingly by the day. She waited by the phone in the dining room for long stretches, hoping against hope that a message would come through. Rumours started coming in that maybe their tank had been hit, but others said it absolutely hadn't happened. We had no sense of certainty. It had been too long not to have heard, but every day there was no word, no word, no word. There was only one thing to do. Two friends of ours—John and Benjy—went searching. They followed the trail of our lost boys; it was the only way we could think of to find something out.

In the end, it was just like in the movies, where soldiers come and knock on your door to give you the brutal news. Shaul, Dudi and our dear blue-eyed Neil had been killed. Was I with Jenny or not when we the news arrived? We were the best of friends. I'm sure we must have been together. But I truly don't remember. I am blank.

Days later, John and Benjy returned with more information. They discovered all three boys had been in the same tank; they'd taken a direct hit and had died instantly. The reason we hadn't heard was because in the mess of this surprise attack, our three friends, who had never been assigned to the same tank, had been hastily jostled in together. There had been no record of this happening in the rush; they had not even been in the same unit before the war. It had taken weeks for the news to be confirmed, but now it was a fact. It could have been any us. But it was them. And just like that, they were gone. All three were 23 years old.

When Des and the rest of the men returned, we were grieving shells of our former selves. The reality of killing and war and of living in Israel had suddenly sunk in. They were people we knew. There was real bloodshed. And one thing was for sure, there was no glory in it, not for anyone; there was only devastation and shock, beyond our imagination. It would hang over us forever. It felt unbelievable, and not a single one of us had the tools to understand it. I couldn't see how any land was worth dying for. I looked at my growing belly and wondered, *If this is a boy, how will I prevent this reality from happening to him?* I kept it to myself, but I knew then and there that if I gave birth to a boy, he would not become a soldier. It wasn't a spoken, explicit decision, it was a secret knowing.

That night, the night Des returned home, I blessed my belly with my tears. Blessed be the memory of the 2600 Israeli soldiers and the 16,000 Arabs who were killed in that war. Blessed be the memory of our beloved Neil, Dudi and Shaul.

# CHAPTER 10

# SOCIALIST MOTHERHOOD

I became a mother in 1974. We named our darling baby boy Nadav to honour Neil, using the first letter of his name 'N' as a sign of respect, as is customary in Jewish tradition. Nadav means 'generous of spirit' in Hebrew, and I loved that. He brought so much joy to our grieving family. He was the most beautiful, perfect creation I had ever laid eyes on. I was in awe. Looking down at new life filled me with so much hope. I had a kibbutz mother's aide assigned to me, Peggy, who visited me every day. She was a lovely lady who helped me with breastfeeding, as well as so many other things. And, quite apart from her, I felt completely held by 'the village'. I had everybody helping me. It felt great. Readjusting to my new body was huge, though, as I thought it would spring back to exactly how it was before the pregnancy. I was naive. But they were blissful times.

Those days moved fast. I blinked and Nadav was six weeks old. This meant I had to hand him over to the kibbutz children's house, six days a week, eight hours a day. I definitely wasn't ready. I didn't know what hit me when I had to leave my baby and go back to work with all those rotten teenagers. But I had nothing to compare it to. It was the norm and it wasn't questioned unless—God forbid—your child was very ill. No one had challenged this way of doing things, as far as I knew. You couldn't live there and do anything else. It was just what you did, and we'd chosen to live there. But it was so painful. And it was traumatic to have no choice.

I was working within walking distance, so I visited my baby many times a day, and was often told I visited him too much. I was too young to know that what I was experiencing was a gaping hole; my body was telling me that I was just not ready for this step. But it was the way of life. I would see him when I was scheduled to breastfeed him. He would be there, lying in his cot, or in someone's arms, or on the floor. I would cry while I was at work; I missed him so badly, but I barely knew what it was I was missing. I didn't know a different way.

By the time I relived this scenario, four years later, with my precious second son, Edo, I knew what was in store for me. But knowing and feeling are two very different things. When I handed him over to the kibbutz nursery, he cried and cried, and it was shocking and heart-wrenching, just as it had been with Nadav. Edo means 'His witness'. I always had the feeling, even when he was such a young baby, that he was witnessing my pain. I held myself together by sending him messages from my heart to his mind. It sounds mad, but it's what I did; it's how I coped. I cherished this private, telepathic connection. That spiritual connection between us continues to this day.

I now had two boys and, of course, the haunting thought of Neil, loved and lost in an unfathomable war, lurked in the corners of my mind. I knew then, somewhere deep inside myself, that I couldn't be in Israel long term. But it was no time to consider leaving. We were all too raw to act on any such thought. For now, we could only hold onto one another.

The next years on the kibbutz were joyous and beautiful. Lots of babies were being born, and it was a time simply to be together. We were living in absolute socialist harmony. We were all equals, we were all cared for, and I've never forgotten that feeling. I still reflect on it, in my work, to this day. We had a wonderful support system, with the nursery and all the families and, despite everything that had happened, it felt like the safest place to have our children. Life on the kibbutz was easy and natural for kids. They were free, and I could not have asked for anything more harmonious, and more starkly in contrast to my own apartheid upbringing. This was the other extreme, and my kids loved it. But the wonder of living on a kibbutz had a shelf life for me. Perhaps it served them well now, but until what age? Somehow, I didn't want them growing up there, and I couldn't imagine them living there as men. I wanted them to have different areas of input, I wanted them to see the 'real world', not just this so-called utopia. I didn't even feel I had the capacity for clear thought from this world inside the kibbutz. We were certainly having a beautiful, fun experience, but as time went on, it didn't feel like a permanent home. I started voicing my feelings to Des, repeatedly.

Des, however, was flourishing. He had found his place, while I was drowning. He'd come home fatigued but fulfilled, after driving trucks all day amid the beautiful golden wheat. He felt he was such a productive part of society. Meanwhile, I came back from a day of folding laundry and being screamed at by unruly children who weren't even mine. I was decidedly frustrated and I tried to express my feelings, but I don't think he heard me. Maybe the roar from the combine harvester he worked on daily had deafened his ears. It was ironic, the very roar that was making him thrive was deadening his senses to me. He continued ploughing those fields, and chose not to believe how serious I was about leaving. It would take another five years before he would listen.

CHAPTER 11

# THE PERM

I was 23 years of age when my sister Margie and I walked into a hair salon in Israel, run by a French hairdresser. We had no idea what hairstyles we were after, we just wanted someone to shake things up, someone who had a vision to do something fabulous to us—anything. Well, Margie walked out looking like a tiger, with incredible golden streaks in her short, jet-black hair. And I came out with a perm. It was the late 1970s, and I don't even remember the hairdresser asking me if he could do it; he just did it. When I looked in the mirror, I gasped. I had a fro of tight curls. I had never felt so beautiful in all my life.

It sounds absurd that a perm could change your life but let me tell you—this perm changed my life! Looking back, it marked a huge turning point. I walked back into the kibbutz that day, and people who had passed me a million times on the path and never greeted me stopped in their tracks and said, 'Wow!' Overnight, I became visible. It actually changed my personality. From feeling like a mouse, hiding in the corner of every social gathering, suddenly I was a woman with a voice. Or at least a woman with an absolutely incredible fro!

I was filled with a new-found confidence. It was a momentous physical trigger for something internal to change. It was time; it felt like an awakening. It felt like freedom from all the comparisons and limitations, from all the years of voicelessness. Suddenly, finally, I had a level of confidence that began to progress and enhance all my abilities. I not only became visible to other people; somehow, in some way, I became visible to myself. I looked in the mirror and for the first time, maybe ever, I didn't see a mouse. I now had a mane. I saw a lion.

Within weeks I was rescued out of my child carer role into an important office job position on the kibbutz. I'd been badgering the equivalent of the kibbutz HR department for years to be moved, and could only suppose that I suddenly looked so amazing that they paid attention! I didn't want to work in an accounts department, but it was definitely better than working with those unruly kids. I didn't have a single skill in the accounts world to make me any good at the job, but somehow I was chosen and championed more or less to become an accountant. Can you imagine? Unfortunately, the perm didn't give me the ability to make sense of numbers. It only meant that I looked pretty good while I was doing it!

I didn't love it. I wasn't inspired, but I became good enough to do it. Though I often found myself doodling in the columns of the ledger book, I took the job on, and gave it my best.

It was around this time that I started really letting myself feel that I wasn't such a good socialist. Let's blame it on the perm, but I was feeling independent and strong. My repressed depressed feelings turned into self-knowledge—I realised I didn't want to be told what to do and when to do it because it was good for the society. I knew for certain that I had been ignoring my feelings and focusing on millions of other things for quite a while. Nine years, in fact. Kibbutz living was working for a lot of people, and had worked for many people for almost a hundred years, but it was suddenly clear that it wasn't working for me.

I wasn't particularly interested in participating, in changing the areas that weren't working for me. I knew I could stay on, join committees, become an active part of the society, push for the changes I wanted to see. Living on the kibbutz was the way to change the kibbutz, and I knew that. But somehow, I didn't want to do it. Who was I to change this society? It was easier for me to leave. I felt for my sanity that I needed to walk away. I grabbed my accounting pad: curly hair plus unfulfilled woman equals time to leave the kibbutz. It was the sum I understood best.

It's strange. Even though I wasn't a good socialist, I still believe in socialism, or at least I believe in a type of socialism. I harbour fantasies of creating a community in my city that is based on equitable sharing, with each person still having their own identity, their own space and work life. Kibbutz living taught me that the form of socialism I believe in is one in which everyone has the right to choose how they want to live, the right to be taken care of by society, and where resources can be shared. There are so many things in a community that you can share. Why do we need twenty lawnmowers on a street with twenty houses? Why do we need forty cars on a street when we could work out a more sustainable transport system? Why do we need twenty swimming pools? Why not share a pool? A veggie patch? A beautiful garden? Why couldn't we create a village that has communal aspects, such as a shared dining room for the people who want it or need it? If you took the best of kibbutz life and put it in a city, then people could choose the work they wanted to do and share the finances accordingly. Everyone would have a roof over their head, security, safety, friends, community, no concerns about money, no thought about their next meal—these were the best aspects of kibbutz living.

But in my fantasy village, if I want to be an artist I should be able to choose to be an artist and earn money. Which is exactly what the kibbutz we lived on has evolved into now, and that is extraordinary. I didn't have the patience to see it through to that place. People said South Africa would change too, and I didn't have the patience to wait for that either. The people who stayed on in South Africa stayed to live through that change. And the people who stayed on the kibbutz got to taste the fruits of their labour. Patience isn't my strong suit. Impatience got the better of me as usual, and turned into action.

One day at work, the number crunching really got to me. That particular day, it seemed obvious that the only thing being crunched was my spirit. I thought, *If I don't pull myself out of this, I'll be buried alive.* I arrived home from work to hear that another kibbutz couple had announced they were leaving. It was all the impetus I needed.

As I was making dinner, I turned to Des and said, 'I need you to know that I can't do this anymore. I've tried, for you. But I have to leave. You either come with us or you don't.' I saw in Des's face that he heard me, for the very first time. It was a powerful moment. He believed me.

He said, 'I hear you. We'll all go.' It was huge. This move would become instrumental for me, for the harmony of our marriage and, following on from that, for everyone in our family. Nadav was nine and Edo was five: both were good ages to transition to new schools. Before I knew it, we were packing up our strange utopian life and moving out into the scary wide world of city living. It felt a brave and courageous thing to do.

After we left, our kibbutz came up with the idea of manufacturing a robotic pool cleaner. An electronics factory had been established while we were living there, to utilise some of the technology skills of the members. This is just one example of the innovation that was prevalent in Israel, even in the 1970s. This new venture was a completely left-of-field idea, because although there were public swimming pools in Israel at the time, there were very few private ones. And yet, completely unexpectedly, this product became a multimillion-dollar business, and made the kibbutz one of the richest in Israel, to this day. It is such a success. Eventually, this financial stability liberated those living there to choose what they wanted to do. It's a very happy place for many people. And that is my prayer for us all—that we are liberated from the constraints and limitations of our lives, able to achieve what it is that we are called to do.

CHAPTER 12

# DANCING FLOWERS

Much like when I left South Africa, where I had never made my own bed or lived without a nanny, when we left the kibbutz in our early thirties, we had never managed our own finances or our own lives before. Money as we know it hadn't existed on the kibbutz, and all our needs had been taken care of. I learnt to like the independence very quickly, but it was pretty scary at first. I was also excited to not have other people deciding what I could and couldn't do with my time, my days, my kitchen, my life. Many of our friends shared this similar, simple satisfaction on leaving. Finally, I could do my own thing!

We moved to Haifa, which was and is a gorgeous, progressive, assimilated city, where Jews and Arabs coexist side by side. But the main reason we chose to move there was that my sister Pam and her husband Geoff lived there. It just so happened that Geoff, who was a doctor of economics, and his friend, who was an artist, had a dream about running a florist shop. So they bought one. But after a short while, they threw their hands up in the air—shopkeeping was not as easy as it looked. They passed the florist business on to Pam, and she found it hard to manage on her own. She offered me a job, and pretty soon we were working together. It was a dream to work with my sister. She did the admin and I did the creative work. Geoff counted the money!

The shop thrived. I didn't know a thing about flowers, but I channelled my thwarted artistic aspirations into strange and wonderful flower arrangements. It was fun. I discovered I was good at it. Flowers were gratifying, and it turned out Pam and I were a pretty good team. I had lots of ideas. I threw in antique furniture; it not only showcased our arrangements beautifully, but offered saleable items that did pretty well. I added beauty products, special jewellery, baskets, vases and ceramics. I filled the shop with everything I loved.

Des found a job managing a squash centre, and pretty soon we were able to rent a nice apartment and do exactly what we wanted on our days off. What a different life from the kibbutz! Neither of us was sentimental, and we only looked forward. We left the kibbutz behind, in our minds. We were here, and we were going to make the most of it. We were focused on surviving, and in this city, we were all able to do it together, whether Muslim or Jew, black or white. The Arab–Israeli conflict was not felt in Haifa. We believed peace would come. We had great hope.

Once the boys were fully settled at school and had made new friends, I really felt we had landed in Haifa, and that was wonderful. Des and I had stable jobs and were both working hard. I started shopping and buying beautiful things, glamorous clothes. I relished each decision I could make with my own money. We went to the theatre and art galleries. We ate out occasionally, and even went to Europe a few times. It was around this period that I also became obsessed with aerobics. From where I was standing, I had a lot covered in my life. Home, health and travel were all sorted. That awareness made me feel that I had the capacity to add value somehow.

I wasn't looking for some special purpose or meaning, but out of the blue this feeling of wanting to give back arose in me, though with no direct sense of how I would achieve it. Then one day, a friend came into our florist shop and told me about a women's refuge that was looking for volunteers. I jumped at it! The refuge was in an obscure little area not far from my work, so one day I just wandered around and found it. It was an Arab women's refuge, for women disadvantaged through a number of different reasons, including domestic violence. Most of them were there with their kids, some were in hiding. This was a transitional housing facility.

I was very excited to find a place where I could offer my services, so I walked in with a whole lot of energy and told them I wanted to volunteer. What would be useful here? What could I do? I asked. They ummed and ahhed for a while, and without much thought I found myself blurting out, 'Would these women like . . . aerobics?' Now, I need to make it clear that my credentials for this of course were that: a) I went to aerobics classes, and b) I loved my pink-and-black Lycra leotard. That was pretty much it. I could barely touch my toes. But much to my surprise, they said, 'Oh yeah! That would be great!' It was the 1980s after all . . .

When the day of my first class came around, I was so nervous that I decided not to wear my aerobics gear. I suddenly felt bad going in looking like a Jewish Jane Fonda in my Lycra leotard and expensive pink Reeboks. These women were coming from brutal situations. It did not feel appropriate to wear all that sporty glam, so I showed up in a rather frumpy outfit. But after the class, a carer walked up to me and said, 'You know, next time, you should come looking the part. It will inspire them. They'll want to do it more.' So I was very excited to walk into my next session dressed top-to-toe in my professional aerobics gear—complete with sweatband, leg warmers, ghetto-blaster and a whole bunch of 1980s hits. I couldn't do a thing in time. Seriously, those two left feet of mine really came to the party. It would've been hilarious to witness. The carers were probably laughing all the way home. But I was having too much fun to be mortified. This had nothing to do with my skills; it had everything to do with my desire to give. I really wanted to do this. Around seven women and their babies or kids would show up, and I'd get the kids involved too, so it was all of us dancing around. It was not exactly aerobics, but it was pretty special. My day job was taming flowers, but at night I made them dance.

I think it was in that shabby room, with my two left feet doing jumping jacks to Cyndi Lauper that I felt, maybe for the first time, what it was like to serve something greater. Suddenly, in that out-of-the-way shelter, all our divisions made no difference whatsoever. We were women, mothers, lovers and children together. We were people looking to find ourselves. And in that hour, we did find ourselves. They found me and I found them. We were sisters, in a country that called us enemies. But enemies did not exist in that room. Wife-bashers did not exist and war did not exist and Neil and Dudi and Shaul were not dead. There was only the simple joy of our spirits flying high and free, while I flipped the tape of 1984 fresh classics again and again.

I danced with my ladies for about six months, until work got really busy. Before I knew it, I forgot to ever go back.

# CHAPTER 13

# EXODUS

As the years moved on, Israel became more and more right wing. The occupation was entrenched, terrorism was hanging over us, and it no longer felt like the Israel we had chosen to live in. The Jews who fled Europe hadn't had a choice. Israel was the only place that would take them unconditionally, because they were Jews. They'd had to go to Israel, come hell or high water. But we had a choice, and we had made the choice to live here. Now that choice was being challenged.

From a personal point of view, though we were comfortable and had some cash, buying property in Israel was a whole other story. There were no loans or deposits for properties in those days. You needed all the cash upfront to buy a place, or you rented. By our calculations, we would never be able to buy a house. Property meant security to me back then, and there was no security like that available to us. Additionally, in 1982, we lived through another war. Des was shipped off once again, and I really couldn't handle it. Then Nadav turned thirteen, and we were facing the looming issue of the army. As soon as he turned fourteen, he would be placed on the Israeli conscription roll, and legally enlisted into military service, no matter what country he lived in, anywhere in the world. Yet if we left while he was thirteen, he would be exempt.

Looking back, our reasons for wanting to leave Israel feel justified. But at the time I was torn by the sense that leaving Israel was a loss and a failure of a longstanding dream. I felt like we were letting the team down, so to speak. But eventually we made the decision, and I knew it was the right one, because my overarching feeling was of relief. But some of our friends were hurt and angry. Ultimately, they were disappointed and took it personally, as if it threw their decision to stay into question. They judged us for leaving, because they were making it work in one way or another. But there was a compelling force within me that was calling, as scary and unknown as that was. I couldn't deny the call to leave, nor could I accept staying as an option. There is something completely heartbreaking about holding on to what you believe in and then realising it's not enough to sustain you. We began looking at moving to Australia. Des had family there. Then, before we knew it, we were lodging paperwork. It was happening.

The boys didn't speak out about not wanting to leave Israel. They never said, 'Please, can we stay,' but it's not as if we gave them a choice. I'm not sure a nine-year-old and thirteen-year-old can comprehend a big move like that. I certainly hadn't understood its many dimensions when I left South Africa, and I had been seventeen. We started preparing them with English lessons, to help them on our arrival, because although we had always spoken to them in English, they responded to us only in Hebrew.

They needed help to be proficient. Every now and then I'd say to Nadav, 'Do you want to talk about the move?' And he'd say, 'Ima [Mum], when I get to Australia, I'll deal with it. Right now, I'm here and I want to be here. Leave me be.' He wanted absolutely no projections about what was coming. Neither of them really wanted to talk about it. But when the time came to give our dog Boomi away to a new family, Nadav hid under a bed. It represented a brutal feeling of heartbreak. That dog embodied all of it—leaving my beloved sister, Pam, our friends, our adopted culture. Boomi the dog gave us all a chance to collapse in grief. Our life as we knew it was ending.

Yes, closing our life in Israel was challenging and painful. I had no idea how we would manage living in Australia, but it did help that some of Des's family had settled there a few years earlier. Margie had also moved to the United States a few years before, and she was flourishing. Surely we would too. I found myself in a constant state of, *Oh my God, I can't believe we're doing this.* We didn't have much money to take with us; we were moving with no jobs in sight and no home set up in Australia. But we spoke English, so that was a big start. And I knew, with absolute certainty, that in order to achieve the security I sought, we would have to dive straight into our insecurity. We would have to swim in it. We would have to get up and leave what was safe and venture into something completely unknown. My greatest heartbreak was leaving my sister Pam. We'd shared every day together. But I was convinced it was the right thing for us. I even had enough belief that I was prepared to carry Des, who wasn't as convinced. But once he hopped on board, he truly did everything he could to make it work.

In that murky sea of the unknown, there was one thing I did know for sure: I wanted to give my children new opportunities, and that didn't include military conscription. It included the right to choose for themselves if they wanted to fight for a country. I certainly did not plan on making that choice for them; they would have to make it for themselves one day. But for now, I would do what I could to protect them. After twenty years in Israel, it was time to uproot ourselves and say goodbye, all over again.

# PART 3

♥

# AUSTRALIA

## CHAPTER 14

# PARTY QUEEN

I have two memories I'll never forget about being new immigrants in Australia. The first one involves Jesus.

Even before our plane had landed, I had put my mind to making sure Nadav and Edo acclimatised to Australia as smoothly as possible. If I could help make this transition easier for them, I was onto it. On arrival, I booked them into cricket camp because I figured this was a very 'Aussie' thing to do. I also booked them into community workshops. I wanted them to make friends and get involved in this new culture that was so drastically different from their Middle Eastern lives. One day in December, I picked up nine-year-old Edo from a pottery workshop. He came running over to me with a big smile and this absolutely beautiful creation in his hands. He was so excited. I took a look at his hunk of glazed clay. It was a lumpen little tent of sorts, with sweet little people wearing tunics and headdresses. I said, 'My darling, what a gorgeous Arab Bedouin tent! How wonderful!'

He looked at me like I was off the planet, and said in his little Israeli accent, 'Ima, what are you talking about? It's Jesus in de manger!' Well, I was in shock, to say the least! The acclimatisation was happening a little faster than I had anticipated. He very rightly put me in my place. It was the cutest thing. I saw Arabs with traditional headdresses (*keffiyeh*), but here was my Jewish son presenting Jesus in the manger. Yep, we were in Australia now! I knew nothing about Christianity or Christmas—there isn't even a word for Santa Claus in Hebrew—but I knew then and there that I was in for a journey of learning new things.

I have another significant memory from around this time. Des and I were carefully discussing the boys' education. We were deep in this ongoing discussion one afternoon—to send them to a Jewish school or not—when fourteen-year-old Nadav piped up and said, 'What is a *Jewish*?' Honestly, I couldn't believe it. I had been so busy focusing on the social norms of our new country that I hadn't even considered the Jewish aspect for the boys. Nadav had never considered his identity. In Israel, we had been Jews in a Jewish country. The society was constructed within the framework of Judaism. There was no place where you needed to explain your Jewishness. Now, we were Jews outside of Israel. From an identity point of view, we would all have to undertake an understanding of what being Jewish meant in this pluralistic country. We would have to work out what that looked like together, as a family. The boys would have to learn that sense of difference. I will never forget looking through his eyes at this transitional time. In the end, we put them into public schools, which felt like the best way to help them become part of their new country.

♥

Moving to Australia was a challenge, albeit an exciting one. Aside from working out who and how to be, we also had to figure out exactly how to survive. Des and I were in our late thirties. Luckily, we stayed with Des's family in the leafy suburb of Chatswood in Sydney, until we found a house to rent in Lindfield, which we did very shortly after arriving. We started looking for work immediately. I was willing to do absolutely anything, except florist work. I'd been there, done that, and it was gruelling work. That career was no longer for me. But it was the end of January, and for some reason, all I could see in the paper were job opportunities for florists! Finally, as Des was not having much luck finding work, I took a florist job in the first week of February, unaware that in Australia February was a very special month in the floral industry. To my absolute surprise, on the fifteenth of February, I was fired. I'd had no idea that I'd essentially been hired for the lead-up to one single day, the busiest day of the year in the floral industry. Valentine's Day didn't exist in Israel 35 years ago.

Almost instantly, I found my next job, as a sales assistant in a lifestyle store. I was selling modern bedding and cushions, and all kinds of home accessories. I didn't like most of the products, and I really didn't like having to ask for permission to do things, but the job fulfilled my interior design fantasies when I was able to make the shop look beautiful. Within a few months, I was given a promotion, which was nice, but I still didn't like being managed. Granted, I had no qualifications but I'd co-run a florist for eight years, so I was used to making my own decisions, including creative ones. Within a year, a family friend offered me the opportunity to run a florist shop. My boss said, 'What's a nice Jewish girl like you gonna do in a florist shop? You can run my beautiful business! I'll make you state manager!' I was tempted for about one second, but had already made my decision to go. I knew I wanted to be my own boss, and even as state manager I would never have the freedom to make the business decisions I wanted to make. My trajectory there was predictable and financially limited. Most importantly, this new opportunity offered me the potential of more money based on my efforts. That was incredibly attractive to me. And exciting! Excitement is always a clue that you're moving in the right direction. It was a stumble into flowers once again, but maybe I was destined to handle smelly vases! I took the job. Within two years there were three florist shops and I was managing them all.

I do love challenges. And I'm (mostly) not afraid of them. When an opportunity is given to me that has the potential to test my resilience, push me in different directions, be independent, face my limits, I simply can't help myself. It's an inner voice that wants me to move forward, and I've learnt to listen to it and trust it. I've often found myself putting my hand up and saying, 'I'll do that!'— even things I've never done or dreamed of doing before. When you take a chance, the gifts find you. You may not succeed, but in my opinion, that's not necessarily the point. There is deep satisfaction and excitement in attempting something unknown. In this case, it paid off. The florist shops did well. And I thrived, despite the three o'clock flower market wake-ups.

One day, I was planning flower bouquets for a wedding, and the bride-to-be said to me, 'I need more.'

'What do you mean?' I said.

'Well, what else can you do?' she asked.

'Oh, do you want me to do flower settings for the tables as well?' I said, unsure what she was after.

Then she said, 'Why don't you come and take a look at the venue?' Well, I'm not exactly sure why I went. I could sense she had money, and I was into making money, so I followed her. I took one look at the venue and, all of a sudden, these words were mysteriously coming from my mouth. Such as, 'We could drape chiffon on the ceilings,' and, 'You could have some fairy lights over there.' I have no idea why I was saying this, but these ideas were popping into my head. My imagination felt unrestrained as to how I could unleash my creativity while very happily spending her money. Suddenly, I wanted to give her the most beautiful event she could imagine, and I was so good at making it all up on the spot.

To my surprise, I designed that wedding. I draped, I tied, I cut, I flowered, I napkin-ringed. I even forklifted! I hadn't any idea what I'd committed myself to doing. I almost killed myself, but I did it and it worked. It was pretty scary, and so much hard work, but I loved it. It gave me so much satisfaction! Needless to say, I left the floristry business. After that wedding, all these other people started calling me to decorate their weddings and bar mitzvahs. And I said yes. I said yes to them all. I said yes a little too often probably, because I seem to remember that I once said yes to nine events in one weekend. You read that right. Nine events. One weekend. Our whole family drove around delivering flowers. Literally. Brother-in-law, sister-in-law, my children, my husband. I had 90 lots of everything for 90 tables. That was intense. I still can't believe I did that. I must have been crazy. I also probably had a few dissatisfied customers. But I do thrive on a bit of crazy.

Things were going pretty well. Especially considering I was making everything in my garage. Everyone wanted something different, and I wanted to provide it. If you needed something, I loved being the one to supply it. I didn't know the word then, but I know it now—I have always been an entrepreneur. My brain is wired that way. It's innate. I decided to call myself Ronni Kahn Party Decorations. I had a funny little business card with balloons on it. It was so low-key. I had my garage, and I had me, myself and I, as well as my family for backup emergency support. Every single client came through word of mouth. I couldn't believe I was doing it. I had my own business.

It certainly wasn't all smooth sailing, though. One of my first events, which I had thought was a dinner, was actually a brunch. So when the caterer called me to tell me the guests were less than an hour away, and I was still in my pyjamas with not a single flower or decoration arranged, I almost dissolved into thin air from the panic. I don't think I've ever had so much adrenalin course through my body at one time. Or ever mobilised myself so very, very quickly! My flowers were all still in buckets in my garage! I literally arrived at the venue while guests were coming in. I dumped hundreds of flowers into their swimming pool and haphazardly tossed full-stemmed flowers on the floor, as though this had been my bohemian plan all along. I got away with it, by the skin of my teeth, but I came terribly close to losing my new business. From that day on, I triple-checked everything, while feeling mildly traumatised.

My first big break came in 1997. I received an out-of-the-blue call from a woman with a thick accent who, as it turned out, was the producer of the Star City Casino opening—Sydney's first casino. I'd never done a corporate gig before, but she asked me to pitch for their prestigious VIP opening. I couldn't believe it. Well, I must have impressed them because I won the job. I'd pitched an *Arabian Nights* themed skyline, with domes and minarets, and it was such a huge endeavour that I'd had to hire my first employee. I was lucky enough to score Colin, an old family friend with great artistic talent. He was so creative, had wonderful taste, and he both trusted and supported my very impractical visions, helping to bring each and every idea to life. I also began to rent a warehouse, to make and house the huge props for this event. I was essentially building a theatre set, with pillars and towers and God knows what. It was insane. To cut a mad story short, we did it. We made their dreams come true and it was amazing. That job opened every corporate door, essentially launching my event career. I now had a track record of coordinating a highly publicised event. I could, officially, deliver: one hundred per cent.

It was only when the gig was done and dusted that, still in a state of disbelief, I asked the hiring producer how she'd heard about me. She said, 'I heard about you from a friend. And, as a woman starting out in the event world in Germany, somebody gave me a break. You seemed very capable, and I wanted to give you the same sort of opportunity I had been given. Well done.' I've never forgotten those words. She paid it forward, and I will always be grateful to her for that.

The events started rolling in and, I must say, there were a lot of sleepless nights after I'd committed to certain ideas. But it was a happy kind of sleepless, because I was crazily concocting ideas. With Colin's help, I once arranged to have one hundred candelabras made. From scratch. We built an ice rink for a bar mitzvah. We had chandeliers made by hand, by an electrician. We—okay, mainly Colin—assembled basketball hoops for fifteen tables. We built a replica of Willy Wonka's factory for a one-year-old. We lined walls in velvet. Sometimes we had animals involved, though 'no animals were harmed in the making of our events', and once we even had a bride in a Cinderella-style carriage. At that time I decided to change the business name to Ronni Kahn Event Design. I loved Donna Karan and everything she stood for, so I decided to be RKED. I felt very special with my new orange-and-black business cards, in my own DKNY reality. It was wonderful.

The business was growing, really swimming along. I loved it. Financially, too, we were in a good place. Des had a great job managing a shopping centre and my business paid well. Finally, we had a deposit for a house. Our calculations showed we could spend $180,000, along with the bank loan, to buy our first home. But the house I really wanted was $250,000. It didn't matter, I settled for less, knowing that in and of itself this represented a huge moment for us. We had finally bought our own house. Then, a few years later, we could borrow more money. We could spend $250,000, but now the houses I really wanted were $350,000. And then a few years after that, we could borrow even more money. We could spend $350,000, but everything we looked at that I absolutely loved was $500,000. Although we finally had some money at our disposal, it always fell short somehow. It seemed the more I had access to, the more I could give myself permission to want. In this case, it didn't seem like my dream house was going to be a possibility.

But I was not willing to give up just yet. I had done my research and discovered that the house I wanted, on the street I wanted, was in Sydney's Bondi Beach. What was available was totally out of our price range, so I had to think creatively. I decided to become my own real estate agent! I would go to that street and knock on the doors of houses that looked shabby enough to possibly be affordable. Maybe someone would be interested in selling. I figured the seller would make more money if they sold directly to me without an agent taking a cut. It seemed we would all benefit. The first door I chose to knock on was the most run-down, unrenovated house I could find. When they finally opened the door, I asked, 'Are you interested in selling your house?' I told them I wasn't an estate agent, which I quite clearly wasn't.

They were an older couple and they said, 'How much would you give us?' I'd done my homework and knew exactly what their house was worth. They looked at each other, looked back at me and said, 'Yes, we'll do it.' And that was that. Finally, *finally*, I had the house of my dreams. Surely, now we could put down our roots and everything would fall into place ...

CHAPTER 15

# NEW SKIN

One day, I received a little parcel with a couple of innocuous-looking face creams from an old kibbutz friend who had moved to America. Her neighbour had asked her who she knew in Australia, and she had said she knew one person. She promptly posted me these products to support her friend. She had no real knowledge of why her friend wanted to give them to me or her reasons for doing so.

I was curious and delighted to be given free face creams, and used them straight away. I'd never really used face creams before. It seemed like a very fancy thing to do and I was excited. One of them was a mask that was supposedly a 'face lift'. I remember it had hyaluronic acid in it. Although I'd never heard of it, the packet said hyaluronic acid was known to be a naturally occuring component of our skin. I lathered it on quick smart, and within minutes the cream went so stiff on my face that I thought something had gone terribly wrong. I thought I might be deformed for life! Then, after I washed it off, I completely freaked out. It was, quite literally, a face lift. I promise you. I looked completely different; I had not one wrinkle.

I was radiant. I looked so much younger! After using it, I walked out of the bathroom and Des said to me, 'Oh my God, what have you done to your face?' Now, my husband was not a guy who noticed things. I could cut off my hair, curl it, dye it, and he would be none the wiser. He had never been one to notice a single thing about my appearance so, based on that, I thought, *Seriously? My God, I have to sell this product, because if he can see this, it must really be something!*

I wrote to the friend of my friend and told her I totally loved these products. And before I knew it, the whole marketing force of that company came down on me. A guy from America came to talk to me. They wanted to sell this product in Australia. But it wasn't to be sold in shops. It was only to be sold through people, through a type of pyramid scheme. I'm not sure I fully understood how it all worked initially, but I was into it because I was completely in love with the product. I could never have sold it otherwise. I became so into it that I travelled to America to meet one of the leaders. He'd made millions selling this product. His house was so cool, and we'd meet there and have these little meetings for a handful of us—all people who, just like me, were at the first level of this thing in their hometown.

I started giving this new little side business a lot of my time. With all the meetings I was attending, all the courses and everything I was learning, a whole world of possibility started opening up for me. I learnt that this new way of selling was called 'Network Marketing'. It gave people the opportunity to start their own business at a minimal cost, selling a great product, directly to customers, without the middle man. By recruiting more people, you earned a percentage of their profits, and when they recruited, they earned a percentage of those people's profits. It meant everyone was leveraging their time in a different way. I just loved that concept. It made so much sense to me. The idea was that the more product people in your group sold, the more everyone in your network would gain. I started sharing the idea of joining this business with everyone around me, and my friends thought I'd gone absolutely nuts. They bought a cream here and there, but they were not really into me experimenting on their face! Beyond all that, however, I was learning something much, much more important.

For the first time in my life, I started learning about the concept of self-belief, and that was something I'd never really heard of before. It was huge for me. Even though I'd succeeded in different ways by this point in my life, that success had unfolded because of a very primal survival instinct within me. My choices had always been driven by functionality, workability, money. That is what I'd learnt from my mother. It was my core programming. There had been little intentionality around it. None of my decisions had considered my personal growth or fulfilment. This company taught us to inten-tionally seize our dreams. The notion they supported was, *You can do anything you want to do. What's stopping you? What stories are you telling yourself that prevent you from following those dreams?* This was a deep process, and I was bowled over. I loved it. I loved learning, and I loved the buzz of all these people I was meeting. For the first time in my life, I opened my mind and my eyes and ears to what I considered really inspirational people. And I was hooked! Hooked on the belief that *you can.*

♥

I'd always lived around practical people, and from them I'd learnt some basic concepts. Lofty aspirations were for the foolish. Work hard and earn what you need. The subliminal message was that anything beyond core needs is, quite simply, a vision of grandeur. I had not been particularly unhappy with this set-up, but I also had no idea there was any other way of living. My parents had never said 'You can be what you want'. Des had never said 'You can be what you want'. No relationship, none of the people around me had said 'You can be what you want to be'. And I'd never found it within myself to tell myself that either. Yet I'd been scrambling in the dark to find who I really was, what I really was, for so long. I had carved out a sense of fulfilment within the work that had presented itself to me, but had I ever allowed myself to choose my path without limitations? Where could that type of thinking take me now that my mindset had shifted?

The product leader for my group, Marc, would say, 'There are fundamentally two types of people in the world: those who *can* and those who *can't*, and they're both right.' That landed on me so intensely. It resonated for me so much, in the sense that it was not just a way of being, but an actual choice. I made the choice then and there to be the person I wanted to be, to be one of the people who *can*. I would never delegate that responsibility to anyone else ever again. Not to my parents, not to Des, not to any other external force.

Stepping out of my comfort zone with intentionality when something lit me up became my new default mindset. I discovered I had the capacity to be passionately influential. I was fervently sharing a message, and because I loved the product I could authentically sell it. Part of my new role was giving pep talks to my team, which was a huge step for me. I was sharing my own words and my own thoughts. Pretty soon I had about a hundred people under me. I loved it so much. Leadership, in this way, felt natural to me.

I remember this one guy, John, who was the blokeyest of blokes, with the biggest beard. I had to demo the facelift on him and had quite a bit of trouble lathering the product on his half a centimetre of non-bearded skin, but I managed. And somehow, I recruited him as a salesperson. To this day, I don't know how I recruited him, but he genuinely loved the product. He was determined to build his own business by selling it. 'John,' I'd say, 'you have to facelift people. That's your biggest weapon.' He certainly tried. He called me one day to say, 'Ronni, I think I've stuck a woman's eyes together. I may have caused permanent damage.' Oh my God, I had such giggles with John, my most memorable hairy beautician. I had so many good times with all these new friends.

What was really changing for me? My horizons. I had suddenly reimagined the potential of my life. I had always chased things, but had not understood my inner power, the capacity of my mind to influence my actions. Now I was changing the way I walked upon the earth. I wasn't just 'doing' anymore. Every step had a whole new resonance. To me it seems no coincidence that it was a skincare brand, because I was absolutely in a process of shedding my old skin. My cells were being regenerated, and not from the hyaluronic acid! Because from that moment on, I never just *did* stuff again. It was as if I understood the 'doing' now. I had an awareness of cause and effect, of the power of the way I thought and spoke and walked in the world. Nothing I did was because I had to or because it was the way it was. It was my choice. It was a beautiful meditation to live in this way.

I began reading all this marketing material, which was really the first motivational literature I'd ever read. It was the first time I was exposed to any kind of self-improvement philosophy. And that material opened the door to books by other motivational people, like Anthony Robbins, Carolyn Myss and Wayne W. Dyer. It became clear to me that I had been starving, though I'd never even noticed I was hungry. Suddenly RKED was changing too. My eyes were opening to a bigger vision. I stopped thinking in a small way. And in turn, my events grew and grew.

I was on a mission to sell this product. I wanted to be rich. I wanted to earn millions. But ironically, although the money was a motivator, I began to be concerned with things beyond the material. There was no blatant spiritual content in any of this marketing material, but in so many ways it was my first 'spiritual experience'. I started connecting with who I was on what felt like an expansive and liberated level, rather than from a place of what people thought I was, or what I'd been told I was, or what I thought I should be. My interactions changed. I treated my clients differently. I heard people's needs in a different way. I parented differently. I listened with different ears. I could connect. I felt skilful in the way I communicated. And maybe none of them would agree reading this, but that was my experience. It was my first experience of touching something deep and fundamental within myself. It was such an important shift and the biggest personal learning experience I'd ever had.

One particular day, after I tried to sell some product to a friend, she turned around and said, 'Ronni, listen, I'm not going to buy your products, ever. I don't use face creams. I don't want to use these. I love you and I'll always be here for you. But enough.' This made me realise

I was truly driving everyone around me completely insane. But from where I was standing, I was doing everyone a favour, because I wanted everyone to be the best they could be and look the best they could while they were at it! I knew my kids absolutely hated it, because it took up a lot of my time, and they died of embarrassment daily because I had become an evangelist. But my husband despised it more than anyone.

I can't say for sure what was really going on for Des, or what he saw, but the truth is I was changing. And not just because my skin was so fresh or because I was deeply involved in a marketing cult. I was changing because all my self-limiting thoughts were fading into the background, and it was filling me with a confidence I'd never had before. My perm twenty or so years earlier had triggered my physical confidence. But now, for the first time, my inside had caught up with my outside. This confidence came from within.

I became utterly immersed in this world of possibility, and it began unravelling us. I believed we could be and could do whatever we wanted. I wasn't exactly sure what that meant, and it's not as if I had something particular in mind, but I had a sense that it meant we could play, we could get creative, we could take action that inspired us and was life-giving. We didn't have to merely stumble along, survive, make do. We could choose things consciously and intentionally if we wanted to.

At this point in our family life, we had reached financial stability and security. I was in my mid-forties and I loved my job. Nadav had finished university already, Edo was in his senior years at high school.

The boys were so grown up, and I supposed we would soon have an empty nest. For me, that meant time to explore new horizons, to be adventurous. I think for Des it meant time to consolidate, not shake things up. Somehow I felt that I had to fight to stay in that new world of possibility. And I get it, I was clumsy with how I went about delivering the message. I'm sure I seemed lost in la-la land. I was totally high on this drug of new potential. But all I was thinking was, *Wow, I can do anything I want. I am not limited.*

It may sound dramatic to say this, but in a way it began the real demise of our marriage. The network marketing didn't ruin us, I simply began changing in a way that pulled us apart. My new world excluded him completely. It was all about me and what I could do. I had been running businesses forever, but my business had never been my life. This new business, however, kind of took over because I needed to be switched on all the time. It wasn't hard for me. I welcomed it. It was the right timing in my life to have something switched on. It just happened to be through this vehicle of network marketing and the new people that I'd met. I suppose it could have been anything. But it was this, and Des didn't get it at all. He hated it, he hated these people, and was convinced they were all phony. The teachers were all American and he felt the whole thing was American hype. I don't think he ever came to a meeting, but he would hear me coming back from them and he just hated how I sounded and how I spoke. From his point of view, I'd gone totally mad. I had become a type of motivational speaker in my own home. God knows, I must have been impossible to live with and terribly annoying.

But it was undeniable: a new power had been unleashed in me, a power I had never known. This whole thing was a life-lift, more than a face lift, and I wasn't prepared to give it up for anyone. Nothing I'd ever been involved in had been about self-improvement or self-empowerment. Everything I'd done was about survival. Every. Single. Thing.

I was now thinking I might want to quit RKED at some point. But I didn't. And the reason I didn't was none of my team were really selling any product and so, though I had a little money moving through, it was only the tiniest income. I started realising I would have to invest a lot of money to make this work. I would have to buy, use and sell a whole lot more product, and so would everyone else. And no matter how much I was inspiring my team—and I thought I was pretty good at inspiring them—it just wasn't happening. The product wasn't selling.

I was at the very beginning of this product coming into Australia. If I'd stuck around, who knows what could have happened. But after investing all that time and energy, I only lasted a couple of years and then left. I never made my millions and leaving felt like failure, definitely. I was embarrassed to face my friends after losing my mind a little bit. But, as strange as it may sound, I mostly felt exhilarated from everything I had learnt about myself. In that regard, I've never regretted this chapter in my life.

The whole experience taught me a lot. I learnt how to rebound from a sense of failure. I learnt how to speak from my heart in a business context, and how powerful that was. I learnt it was up to me to decide what to pour my precious energy and power into, that I had the capacity to bring about the things I wanted to see. But most importantly, I learnt that there were possibilities in my life. All I had to do was open myself up to them.

## CHAPTER 16

# KEYS TO NOWHERE

I've always liked solving problems. Not mathematical ones, social ones. I'd solved people's wedding problems, I'd solved my money problems through my event management business, and I solved our house problems. I've always had an inflated idea about how good I am at solving things. It's probably completely disproportionate, but I do in fact fix things quite well. I don't like shying away and saying, 'It's not my problem.' If you involve me, I'll get right in there, maybe to my, or your, detriment! Somehow, I feel responsible for things, for people, for solutions, whether it's called for or not. And this fix-it compulsion—when it's channelled in the right way—can be really powerful. But I have also worn my 'fix-it hat' in the wrong place several times in my life. I tried to fix my husband, almost without noticing, because I wanted him to change. But loving someone means accepting who they are and not requiring them to change. I didn't have the understanding to realise that then.

It happened so insidiously, but before we knew it, Des and I were living parallel lives. This was probably a year or so after I'd left network marketing. We'd now been in Australia for about twelve years. We'd had quite the journey. During that time, we'd begun a completely new life in a new country with new jobs. We had shed our socialist lives, our Israeli lives, and now we were really living our Australian life; we'd done it. There was so much to be proud of. And, for the first time, our family had what felt like 'real' security. We had just moved into our newly renovated dream home, the house I'd really, really wanted. We'd worked so hard, we'd put so much focus and energy into fixing it up and building our business lives and securing the perfect place for the family, but we had completely forgotten to invest in our relationship. I regret deeply that it didn't work for us, but at this point I couldn't fix it. It was a great failure.

Days after Edo graduated from high school, I remember being alone in the house on a very grey afternoon. Des had gone to work and the boys were out. There I was, standing in my dream house, when I suddenly realised I wasn't in my dream house because this was not my dream. There was only the deepest loneliness I'd ever felt. And even though the house had my stamp in every corner of every room, beautiful things I'd sourced and loved and bought, it was just a house now. A shell of something. An echo. I went to my drawer and grabbed a bunch of clothes. I honestly didn't really know what my feet were doing, but I let them carry me. It was an out-of-body experience. I remember closing the door of our freshly renovated home, into the black unknown. I felt guilty, elated, mixed, torn, justified, powerful, completely confused, but driven. I carried that cluster of clothes in my hands and put them in my car. I remember holding my bunch of keys tightly in my hand, only to realise they were keys to nowhere now. I was leaving my marriage. It was a lone act of madness; I had not planned this for this day at this time. But it was the only thing my body knew how to do.

These days, when friends, especially younger friends, tell me they are leaving their partners I say, 'I've been there, and I now know that freedom doesn't necessarily come from leaving. Leaving doesn't necessarily even make anything easier, especially if there are young kids involved. The freedom you are seeking is going to come from a bigger, deeper process within yourself. Please, think this through carefully.' Please understand that I'm not talking about abusive or dangerous situations. I'm referring to relationships between two people that are worth saving, and they deserve doing everything in your power to work it out. The repercussions of dividing a family are not easy. They are never easy, even now. No one told me that. I don't think it would have changed anything if they had told me; I probably would not have listened. But no one did tell me. I landed on Colin's doorstep with those few useless belongings in my hands and I tried to think how I would assemble my new life as a single, middle-aged woman. Colin ushered me through his door, gave me his shoulder to cry on, his couch to sleep on. He was my trusted old friend and his home was a safe place.

Not long after leaving the family home, I volunteered for a social organisation. My job was to take people to hospital who had no one to take them—not emergency situations, just regular appointments and support. One day I took this elderly lady to hospital. She said to me, 'Are you married?'

'No, I've actually just left my husband,' I said.

'Ohh, did he beat you up?'

'No, no,' I said quickly, 'he's a very good man.'

'Was he terrible to the children?' she asked.

'No, no, he is great with the children.'

'So, what's wrong?' she said.

She could not understand how I could leave someone who was a nice person, a good man and a good father. I could understand how for her—a woman whose husband had beat her and left her body very frail—it seemed an insane decision that I had left. I could not explain my situation to her. I could not explain the complexities in my mind. I could barely articulate it to myself. But after I dropped her at the hospital, I found myself crying the whole way home.

## CHAPTER 17

# PRINCIPESSA

This chapter of my life that I'm about to share is something I have never talked about publicly. In fact, there are parts of it that I have completely blocked from my mind. I'm quite good at blocking things out; I recognise that now. It's one of my coping mechanisms. I know I have done this throughout my life, during particularly difficult times. I could make a guess that it began when Florrie left, or when my dad had his terrible accident. Regardless of the reasons, I'll slowly try to retrieve it, the bits that I can. I feel I must do so, because it contains critical information that has bearing on the events that followed in my life.

Not long after my marriage ended, I met Anton (not his real name). Anton was an American who was also in the hospitality industry. He knew how to navigate all worlds beautifully, and he attracted me in so many ways. He was worldly, thoughtful, travelled, rich, and saw in me things that no one had ever seen. Much to my surprise, my kids didn't like him, and then my friends didn't like him either. They all saw something else in him. They thought he seemed phony and inauthentic. But to me he was just like Cary Grant: the ultimate elegant gentleman, a charmer, and though this will sound creepy, he reminded me of my father in that way. He had all the trimmings of elegance. He was cultured and generous and, in a nutshell, was everything I thought I had always wanted in a man.

Life with Anton had no limits. We saw every play, every exhibition, anything that was anything from a cultural point of view. He would organise impetuous, spontaneous experiences, such as randomly picking me up in a limo, just for fun. My birthday presents were going to Armani or Tiffany's, and picking out whatever I wanted. Once, he flew me to Hong Kong for dinner. He would go to extreme lengths for us to experience things deeply, like his love of music and opera. And even though my life before Anton had reached what felt to me like a pretty comfortable place financially, I'd never been in a limo in my life. And though my love of shopping was always well nurtured, I'd never bought anything that wasn't hanging on a sale rack. He opened my mind to a new, material world. I'd never lived this way before. I'd never let myself have such luxurious things. I'd certainly never felt deprived, but I'd never felt spoilt or pampered, by myself or anyone else. For a girl who was raised by practical parents, lived on a kibbutz and had always worked hard to save and get ahead and make things happen, I was now in absolute heaven. Suddenly, I was living a fairytale, just like Julia Roberts in my favourite movie, *Pretty Woman*. The princess and her prince. I'd grown up with those stories. And that's just how I felt. He treated me like an absolute princess in every possible sense. His name for me was even *principessa*, which enchanted me even more.

Anton had a dream for me. He told me continually, in many different ways, that I was spectacular. He saw a brilliance in me that I could scarcely understand. He had so much ambition for me, ambition I'd never even dreamed of for myself. I sat back and watched him dream up all these ideas for me. He had enough dreams for both of us. Apart from my network marketing people, I'd never had anyone believe these kinds of things about me. I felt that the things I was good at had always been taken for granted in my life, and the things I wasn't good at had been emphasised. For the most part, I'd quite agreeably gone along with this, believing 'this is my story; this is my lot'. But this guy just saw absolute greatness. It was amusing and endearing. It was unbelievable and completely magnetic.

Anton wanted me to be the queen of the event world. Initially, I thought he simply wanted me to have greater financial security. But he wanted more than that. He wanted me to be on the pages of all the papers. He was always saying, 'Here's what we're going to do.' And I loved that. I had always been the decision-maker in my marriage, and my husband had needed convincing about absolutely everything. I'd never realised how much I'd craved being taken care of in this particular way. I wanted to lean on a man in that way. It became a deep, sometimes guilty, pleasure.

I realised something wasn't quite right very soon into the relationship, maybe six months in. I was driving through the city on my way home, when I saw Anton walking on a busy Sydney street. I had finished work early that day, and I thought it would be fun to surprise him. I picked up my phone and called him. I watched him pick up his phone from a distance, and then I said, 'So, where are you?' as a kind of cute thing because I was going to do the big reveal that I was right there, that I could see him.

'I'm in Lakemba,' he replied.

'No, seriously, where are you?' I asked.

He repeated again, 'I'm in Lakemba, and I'm just leaving work.'

If you don't know Sydney, Lakemba is a suburb nowhere near the city centre. I pulled him up on it straight away. 'Have you done this to people before, that you lie about where you are? I'm here! I can see you!'

He simply said, 'Nonsense! I'm in Lakemba, and I'll see you later.'

I never found out what Anton was doing that day, but I was quite disturbed by the incident. I honestly can't remember how he weaseled his way out of that one in the coming days. But there was something so eerie about the way he had sounded that afternoon, even beyond the lie. I do remember that I told him not to come to my house that night. I suddenly knew, deep down, that I didn't know this man. I felt a strange, sinister feeling. He was untrustworthy. But I wanted to make it work so badly that I was willing to overlook those feelings. I'd never been alone. I was afraid to be alone. So, I stayed, and I kept staying, even as many strange things followed.

Slowly but surely, I discovered more about Anton that did not add up. The pieces just fell into my lap, I never even had to look for them because I was never particularly suspicious. But what I didn't want to see became impossible to ignore. Eventually I found out from one of the only friends he ever introduced me to that he had been married five times, yet he'd never told me. In fact he was still technically married, albeit separated. I found out he had two grown sons that he'd never mentioned. I found out he'd lied about his age—he'd told me he was five years older than me, but in fact he was eighteen years older. I found out all the money he was using to splurge on me was not really money he was making, but money he'd saved or 'acquired' somehow. He was not rich, and pretty soon he was going to be in deep financial difficulty.

Whenever I confronted Anton about any of the lies or omissions I'd uncovered, he felt no need to explain why he'd lied. He didn't win me over with big explanations or vulnerability. I found that more fascinating than anything. He owned everything, all his lies, all his flaws. And no matter how distraught I was, he never apologised. It always ended up being a problem that I had to come to terms with. Every lie was presented as irrelevant in the face of his love for me. I bought it all, not because he had a way with words, but because he knew how to weave a web. There was something sticky about it all. I distinctly remember feeling I was being woven, or reeled in and reeled out. And deep down, I think the way I bypassed all of this was by thinking that I could change him somehow and make him a more authentic, honest person. I still hadn't learnt that lesson. Or maybe it was the opposite. Maybe it's that I thought he could change me, make me special somehow. I think I wanted both.

I told no one the truth about the intricacies between me and Anton, and I simply made myself believe everything I wanted to believe. I overcame so many of the difficulties because he brought something abstract and compelling to the table, that made me feel able to overcome anything. Ironically, he created a feeling of safety for me. He could make everything magically feel okay. And he never made me feel sorry for him. I liked that he was strong enough to just be who he was—totally flawed, and accepting that that's who he was. I understand now how people can love a person who does awful things. He was far, far from perfect. And yet, whatever the package contained, I was willing to put up with it. I wasn't a better person with him—I was more superficial—and I knew it. But I thought it would be okay, for a little bit.

Time continued on with Anton. Break-up after break-up, we kept staying together, and I kept letting myself be blind and euphoric and he kept being the (flawed) Prince Charming I had been waiting for my entire life. We continued our wild decadence and shopping and parties, and what I felt was love and spontaneity, and he continued to surprise me and give me access to a world I had never entered before. I suppose I must have believed I couldn't have that world without him.

Maybe it's a cliché, but somewhere amidst this warped fairytale of 'Principessa Ronni' I started to feel obnoxious. It became embarrassing when he'd pick up my unassuming friends in a limo just to go to dinner. He'd pay for everything, just throw his money around. Another overseas trip, another pair of Manolo shoes; his behaviour no longer made me feel glamorous, it made me feel uncomfortable. I don't think anyone at the time noticed this new cringe within me. Outwardly, I was still functioning as my bubbly self. But a veil was being lifted. I felt bloated and overindulged, and a rising dread started to take hold of me.

When a friend of mine came to stay with us from overseas, things took a really bad turn. While he was seemingly so accommodating, he actually became insanely resentful of my time with her, of my hospitality and her presence. One night, he just lost it. He insulted her in a huge outburst, leaving us both aghast and me humiliated.

I felt utterly mortified. Something died inside me; I never felt the same way about him again.

Soon after, I woke up with something weighing on my mind. I had noticed large quantities of really beautiful food going to waste in my work and I thought, *Why can't we take this and make it useful? Feed people! How hard can that be, for goodness sake?* Over breakfast, I casually mentioned to Anton the potential for doing something about this. His response was immediate and unflinching, and I will never forget his answer. 'I don't believe in acts of charity,' he said.

You'd think I would have got the message much earlier that things did not add up with Anton. But this precise incident was a real moment signifying the end. It was that punch-in-the-gut moment, when you know for certain that you are with the wrong guy. Our values could never align: that was the understanding that landed in me, in that simple interaction. And it's not that I knew how I would feed people with leftover food. But when he rejected the concept of spending energy on others—what he called 'charity'—it completely undid something inside me. For Anton—this was clear to me now—there was no intention of ever doing anything involving anyone beyond himself, beyond us and our comfort and pleasure. He wasn't indifferent or ignorant or uninterested—he was actually *against* helping others.

I looked around our house. We had more than enough of everything. I couldn't help but ask myself, *What do you do if you have enough? What is enough? And what can you really do for other people anyway?* It struck me that morning that I had spent so much time looking after myself that I had become completely self-absorbed. The person I'd wanted to be after I left my marriage, the person I'd planned to be based on everything I'd learnt through my network marketing self-development phase, had amounted to nothing. How far from my values had I fallen with this man? How mesmerised had I become with glamour? What had I really been running away from? How had I become so unaligned with my values, so utterly cosseted, that I was in a relationship that completely warped my principles? Finally, I heard all the alarm bells that had been ringing for my sons and friends throughout the years, loud and clear. From where I was standing, Anton and I were now absolutely over. The question was, when and how?

Not long after this interchange, Anton had a small medical procedure that required an overnight hospital stay. All had gone well, and when I went to visit him in hospital after the surgery, I saw these pretty flowers by his bed. 'Where are the flowers from?' I asked.

He answered, 'Ah, they were just here.'

'That's interesting,' I said, 'hospitals don't usually just have hand-picked flowers.' But he brushed it off, as usual. Suddenly, this woman I'd never seen before walked into the room with eyes only for Anton. She went straight to him, bright and smiling—she didn't even notice I was there—and embraced him. They were clearly well acquainted. There was an intimacy between them.

'Who is this?' I said out loud. She looked at me, and then at him. I asked again, 'Who are you?'

She mumbled, 'Umm, err . . . Who are *you*?'

'I'm Anton's partner,' I replied. 'But don't you worry. I'm out of here.' I grabbed my bag and walked out.

By now I knew very well that Anton was the kind of guy who didn't leave anyone until he'd found a replacement. He'd sensed my withdrawal and was never going to let himself be left behind. I drove home, feeling strangely calm. I went on his computer to verify what I'd seen, and found his romantic emails to her. It was clear the poor woman had no idea he was with me; I could see that. He was doing to her the same thing he'd done to me. She was as clueless about his life as I had been. We had been together for seven years. It was enough. This man of mine, he was a very brilliant con man.

I sent him a text that simply said, 'Where do I send your things?' I called one of my close friends and told her what had happened. 'I'll be there,' she whispered into the phone, and within minutes she was packing up all his belongings with me. The way I boxed his things was the equivalent of throwing everything out the window or onto the yard, with no care whatsoever. I was just hurling his things into boxes. I felt drunk with freedom. Yet I was meticulous. I wanted no trace of him left.

He wrote back. 'How can you do this?'

'Very easily,' I responded. 'You are not stepping into this home ever again.' He probably had a heart attack from the shock, so luckily he was still on that hospital bed! I wasn't in the most caring place by that point. It was our last interaction, and the first time I'd felt strong in a very long time. My power had been locked away, hidden within his power for so long. I regained myself. The spell was broken. There was so much relief. It was the end of the Anton chapter for me. But it wasn't quite the end.

Anton started stalking me. I'd find his card on my windshield, everywhere I went. He would send me messages that he would kill himself if we didn't get back together, and take others down with him. AVOs (apprehended violence orders) followed, and, oh boy, what a mess I'd gotten myself into. I'd been with this guy for years, someone I suddenly realised I'd barely known. I'd gone all out with this skin-deep way of living. I felt like I had sold my soul somewhere out there, and I've judged myself harshly for it over the years. But I do know that if Anton hadn't happened, I would not be the person I am today. He catapulted me into an unquenchable desire for meaning, and that decadence and self-gratification he had nurtured became a gateway, one that made me unable to continue on the path I had been on. Somewhere inside that sickly-sweet indulgence, I landed in a very real place.

The reason I never share the Anton chapter in my talks is that I still feel so much shame. The story displays my superficiality at its height, and it's not the most flattering picture, I suppose. I did love the man—I really did. But I'm embarrassed that I fell for someone so vacuous and troubled; I'm embarrassed that I hung around for so long; I'm embarrassed that I became equally vacuous. Maybe I fell in love with the way he took care of me. If I'm honest, on some level I knew there was something wrong from the very beginning, and I chose not to look at it. It's not that I didn't see it. I just didn't know it enough to act on it. I think that's the source of my shame.

Ultimately, my guess is that Anton wanted to be special himself. He wanted to be special in a material sense. He wanted all those glamorous things for me so he could be the accessory to that special thing. And yet somewhere inside that web, he showed me what it felt like to be special, albeit in all the most outrageous of ways. To be clear, it's not that I needed to believe I was special to go on to do something great in my life. But there is no doubt that his unequivocal belief in me fundamentally changed something about how I perceived myself. It brought me to understand that there was a light within, one that I was born with, one that had nothing to do with materialism, popularity, beauty or fame. It was simply the radiance of who I was in my essence. A universal, unique essence. The light that's in all of us. I wish I had not had to learn these lessons in this particular way, but I wouldn't give up one vacuous moment if it meant I would miss out on what I've discovered since I met him. Because he, us, whatever it was we had, led me to where I am now, to places within myself I could never have imagined before that experience.

I didn't know the part of myself that wanted to be a princess until Anton treated me that way. All the feelings of not being special and being unfavourably compared to others were still living just under my skin. I was, unknowingly, living in that wounded space and Anton satisfied the part of me that had felt utterly unworthy for so long. After all is said and done, he somehow helped me move from a level of 'this is the car I want, this is the house I want, this is the handbag I want', to a completely new place. Somehow, in some way, those desires expanded to include things outside of just myself. That was the shift after Anton. It was fundamental. Suddenly, there was more to life than just me. And the power I gained when I left him was not the girl-power of having finally walked away. It was the long-awaited quiet understanding that my power was very simply my voice in alignment with my actions and values. I was empowered after Anton because the shock of who I'd allowed myself to become turned into the exquisite pleasure of knowing the kind of a person I wanted to be.

My desire to be of service wasn't uncovered through Anton. It was awakened there. Charity was the opposite of anything I had ever thought about, but the whole Anton chapter made me want to bite into something so real that it was painful. It made me re-evaluate my whole life. I had to reforge my independence—physically, mentally, spiritually. I had to work for that, and from it I came to realise that everything I really needed was right in front of me. And now, as I write out this painful, reprehensible chapter in my life, I see that part of this story is now the experience of owning it once and for all. As I remember it, I'm simultaneously letting go of the shame I've carried, and standing by the part of me that simply did not understand a better way to act. This difficult part of my life has been repurposed. This is alchemy.

My goodness. I'd been so profoundly asleep. But in that slumber, Anton saw a light—my light—and in seeing that light, he ignited something in me. He saw a spark in me that I'd never trusted, and that, in the purest sense, is the spark that's in all of us. That pure vision he had of me has never left me. Wisdom, light and understanding can sometimes come out of the darkest places. And so it was that a con man paved the way for me to shine my light.

# CHAPTER 18

# THE NIGHT THAT CHANGED EVERYTHING

After the Anton fiasco, I found myself at a crossroads. Although I was fully functioning—I had my business and I had my sons—suddenly, in my early fifties, I had to face a dreaded feeling of aloneness. More importantly, I found myself re-evaluating my values from scratch. I'd lived an inauthentic life with Anton. I felt ashamed to have fallen for all that. My sons moved on and my friends forgave me for being so foolish. But what I now knew was that I wanted to take what I'd learnt over the past seven senseless years and find a truly meaningful way to live. Although I'd come out of a completely mad chapter, I actually felt authentically at peace. It was over. I had escaped something frightening with Anton and, in many ways, it had been a long time coming. And though I was at a confronting place in my life, I simultaneously felt eligible, independent, attractive and strong. I had all the trimmings of a materially successful life. I was undaunted. Undaunted enough, perhaps, to open myself up to the possibility of a new venture.

During this strange collapse of my life as I knew it, my event design company continued to do well. All my passion and energy was being channelled into creating beautiful events for people. RKED was a very personal brand. People who took me on were choosing to work with *me*. More than the actual event, I loved meeting my clients, coming to know them and earning their trust. I prided myself on knowing I could sell anybody a dream, and then deliver it. They would say, 'I want a fairytale,' and I would say, 'I'll give you a fairytale.' They trusted me. I was totally pushing the limits of what was being done at the time. I loved most of all the sense of creating without limitation. No one else was doing that. How about an ice-skating rink in a ballroom? How about real peacocks parading in a hotel? Sure, let's do it. Absolutely nothing was too much trouble, even cleaning up the peacock poo, an unexpected repercussion of a crazy idea.

For seventeen years I created extravagant and exquisite events for people, and I loved it. And every single day of those seventeen years, at the end of the event, we threw all the leftover food in the garbage. We tried to divide a few things amongst ourselves. I would always bring stuff home, and all the staff could take whatever was left over to their homes. But there was way, way more than we could take. The caterers weren't so fussed about this. When I'd say to them, 'This is ridiculous, can we do something with all this food?' They'd say, 'It's too hard.' Then there was the problem of containers. How would we package it all? And the other problem was that they were terrified of the potential liability. Every time, we threw all that beautiful food away, every single event, every single day, for seventeen years. It was millions of kilos. It was awful. It was a terrible, terrible feeling.

But soon enough it becomes habitual, so you do it, and you push through the obscene feelings.

Then one night, in 2002, I coordinated an event that was fated to change my life forever. I had landed a huge corporate gig. It was a half-a-million-dollar affair. I was catering for 1000 people—it was one of the biggest things I had ever done, and it was very exciting. With so many guests, I decided to set up stations with food, for easy access. There were cartons of oysters, wheels of parmesan, whole watermelons, barrels of beer and vats of wine: everything was displayed like a Roman banquet and was duplicated at each station so that nobody would have to line up. It looked incredible. Finally, all the people arrived—there was entertainment, there was glorious food, everything was happening—and they had the best event ahead of them. But, before I knew it, the crowd became so drunk, so quickly, that barely a morsel of food was touched. Most of the food I had thought they would eat just wasn't eaten. By the end of the evening, it was insane. I literally had whole stations of food left untouched. It was shocking. *This is out of control*, I thought. *I just can't throw all this food away*. I was well and truly fed up with the status quo. It was the enormity of the waste that night that was different: it changed everything.

Now in terms of my living practice, at work and at home, I was a waster. I had never really heard about or considered issues of sustainability, so I wasn't coming from that place at all. I didn't understand anything about landfill. There was very little awareness of these issues among the general public in 2002. I was not in any way an environmental warrior. All I knew about wasted food was that throughout my entire childhood, when I left food on my plate, my mother would say, 'Eat up, there are children starving in China.' We were in Africa, for God's sake! I probably could have taken my leftover peas to my street corner! Isn't it mad that wherever we live, we assume hunger is happening in another country, instead of in our own backyard?

This was the only aspect of food waste I knew. In no way did it occur to me that the waste before my eyes was having an impact on the planet. These days, I'd like to think the world is waking up, and I'd like to think that's partly from the work OzHarvest has done. Now we understand how intricately connected people and the planet really are. And we know that there will be no people if we wreck our planet. It sounds hard to believe now, but I didn't know that then. But this particular night, the problem was so immense that I saw it. My eyes opened up to something that had been there all along. All I could think about was that I had this beautiful untouched food, and I didn't want it to go to waste. I wanted it to feed people. I wanted to do something with it that felt good. I wanted to know how I could repurpose it.

That night, after the event was over and we'd cleaned, and bumped out, and done a million other things, I was acutely aware that I had a problem on my hands with all this food. I was aware there were hungry people in Sydney. At this particular event, the food was all in cartons—cartons of fresh fruit and veggies and so much more—so from a packaging point of view, it was easy to give it away to someone. What to do? I suddenly remembered a homeless shelter that I drove past on my way home every day. Ironically, it was tucked away behind a Ferrari and Porsche dealership. It was the only one I knew. So I did the only thing I could think to do: I bundled up all that food and started heading there, not even sure if this was something you were legally allowed to do.

I arrived at about three in the morning and there were people of all shapes and sizes milling around, waiting for a space to come up in the shelter. And here I was, arriving in my red convertible sports car, stepping out with huge trays of gourmet food that I was juggling while wearing stilettos. I had to step over sleeping bodies to get to the front door. I felt like such a privileged shmuck.

I rang the doorbell and waited for a reply. Finally, someone opened the door and I said, 'Is this okay, to bring you food?' They said, 'Of course it is!' They opened the door and I brought a few cartons in. They helped me bring in quite a few loads; I had so much jammed in my car. And that was it. When I drove out of there, I was stunned. It was so easy. Fundamentally, I had the capacity to do this after every event. We were never going to have to waste food again. These people could actually use it. I have such a clear vision of that night; it was the night that changed everything.

# CHAPTER 19

# CUPCAKES REPURPOSED

The very next day I excitedly phoned the shelter I'd visited and asked if I could deliver food as often as I wanted, and they said yes. I had no idea that there were thousands of similar charities, I only knew about this one. I thought I'd take everything to them, forever. Later on, of course, I understood that there are intricacies in how it all works. Though that shelter was gracious and grateful, eventually they said to me, 'Look, if you don't have 300 rolls, it's really hard if you bring us 50, because some people are left wanting. We can't just give some people this and not others. It becomes a problem.'

So I had to find smaller shelters to cater for that. I started looking for other shelters, but these places were hard to find. I called the council for a listing of all the shelters in Sydney, and they said, 'Sorry, we don't have a list.' Can you believe it?! They really didn't have one. I had to ask at the shelters themselves where other shelters were. I really only wanted to donate to local shelters, because it was hard to drive far after a big shift in the wee hours of the morning. But when

I dropped the food off safely at any of my newfound places, I felt so elated, so inspired and so useful.

It was now clear to me that I was going to continue with my rogue food deliveries. I had a food waste problem and I had created a very immediate solution that was working for me: I'd simply gather up the food at the end of an event and deliver it to the closest shelter in town. It was easy, and it felt so good. Trays of grilled fish, bread rolls, salads, gourmet desserts—you name it. At this point it was simply a solution for me and my business. Then one day I went into my local health-food store, which made fresh food, and out of curiosity I asked, 'Do you ever have surplus food? And they said, 'Oh my God, yes, right here, right now.' And they gave it to me, there and then. I simply took it with me! And then, wherever I did my shopping I'd ask, 'By the way, what happens to your leftovers?'

'Oh nothing, we just throw it out,' they'd reply.

'Well, what if I could take it?' I'd ask.

And they'd say, 'We'd love that, sure! Come back tomorrow.' A shift was taking place. Our collective mindsets were beginning to be repurposed.

I now knew that there was more leftover food than just *my* leftover food. If I had this much beautiful food going to waste, it made sense that a lot of other people must have great food going to waste too. I thought, *Okay, I want this solution to grow.* At that stage I didn't know about Food Bank and the incredible work they do, but they were not rescuing fresh food and delivering direct to individual charities. In fact, it became clear that no one was rescuing and delivering the quality fresh food that was available from gourmet events, delis and restaurants. Wagyu beef and salmon for the homeless was unheard of and quite a thrill.

Needless to say, the staff at the shelters couldn't believe the quality of the food. They'd been serving sausages, mashed potatoes and white bread for so long that they'd forgotten what other food looked like! It was what they could provide within their budgets. Eventually, once OzHarvest was established, I realised we had to start teaching the staff how to use our produce. Back then, a lot of the staff in shelters were volunteers. They'd never worked with this kind of quality produce. They knew what to do with bangers and mash, and that was it. They didn't know how to use good cuts of meat or beautiful fresh fish. That's why our first OzHarvest program was NEST (Nutritious Education Sustenance Training). A beautiful marketing guy who worked with us—Karl—who had experienced homelessness as a young person, used to say that NEST really stood for 'Nice Easy Simple Tips'. I loved that. We were able to roll out programs to teach carers how to turn beautiful produce into nutritious meals. And, of course, there are still places that only like taking white bread because that is what their clients like. They don't want fancy sourdoughs or olive bread. But I'm getting ahead of myself.

In those early renegade delivery days, in 2002, cupcakes were in vogue. It was the very beginning of those cupcake bakeries. And I was ordering cupcakes left, right and centre. Every event wanted them. And sometimes the place I'd order from would call me and say they had six leftover cupcakes, so I'd travel to pick up six cupcakes and drive them from one end of Sydney to the other. But sometimes they'd call me to say they had 60 leftover cupcakes. That made a lot of people happy. Cupcakes are easy to repurpose! Sometimes the bakeries even wanted to make cupcakes especially for me, and decorate them too. Just because they wanted to give! I used to drop food off at a women's shelter in those days, and the women from the shelter would come and help me put the food away. We'd sit around the kitchen and chat for a while, sometimes over these cupcakes. It was so special.

Around this time, I started asking myself some questions. I loved what I did in my work life at RKED. It was my passion. I loved working for my clients and delivering fairytale events. I did it well and I enjoyed it. It was satisfying, and kept me incredibly energised. And it supported me financially. But repurposing food started getting under my skin. It was so compelling. It felt amazing to be doing something useful and helpful for people who needed it. I also started to feel I couldn't authentically talk to one more person who was putting more significance into purple ribbons, purple drapes and purple invitations, than into their relationship and the life they wanted to create together.

*What is meaningful to me?* I asked myself one day, driving home from another wedding. What have I been created for? I'd definitely asked myself a million times what the world could offer me, but now I was asking what I could give to the world. I decided there was a missing piece in my life. If I died today, what would I leave behind?

I was ready for something, but I certainly wasn't prepared. I didn't have a food-rescue game plan. I'd never had any ambition to start a charity or be in the not-for-profit space. Never. In fact, even though I was now driving food to shelters, I didn't realise I was beginning to set something up. And if I was, I certainly didn't know what it was that I was setting up. Was this charity? Was I creating the very thing that had unravelled Anton and me? All I knew was that it made so much sense. I was following an urge, a thrill. I had food and there were hungry people. If this was charity, then it felt good. It felt more than good. It felt miraculous. I followed my gut and my intuition.

By 2003, I had, in a very unofficial sense, begun a food-rescue operation. I didn't have a name or anything, I hadn't reached that point yet. I was too busy. It was just me, and sometimes my sons and their girlfriends—and of course I roped in Colin—in my RKED van, delivering food very late at night after a big day of whatever party I was coordinating. It was a thing now. I never threw food in the trash again, after any of my events, and the charities welcomed the food with open arms. It was a great way to end a day's work. And it was instant, this falling so deeply and utterly in love with the useful feeling of feeding people.

# CHAPTER 20

# ELECTRIFYING SOWETO

One fine November morning, in 2003, I found myself with a break in my calendar, which was rare. I was delighted. Summer was coming, my busy period at work was just around the corner and I had done all the preparation in advance. It was the calm before the storm, and I decided to embrace my freedom. By this point, my parents had passed away, Pam and her family were still in Israel, and Margie and her family had moved to California. I could have gone to see my sisters, I could have gone anywhere in the world to take a break, but South Africa was calling. I felt a strong need to see my (adopted) family—the Browdes, Selma and Alan—whom I'd seen only a few times over the years on their visits to Australia. I was so excited by the sense of going back to my roots, seeing the old neighbourhood and the old faces. I hadn't been back since Mandela had been freed. I hadn't been back in twenty years. A lot had happened politically. I called Selma and said, 'I'm coming to South Africa! I'll be with you on the weekend.'

And she said, 'Okay, great, but I have to visit a few friends in Soweto on Saturday, and you will come with me.' Soweto? There and then, quite simply, I froze. I had never been to Soweto. I had never been to Soweto because Soweto was completely out of bounds when I lived in apartheid South Africa. I imagined it to be the scariest place in the entire world. Soweto was a black township—which in the South Africa I knew meant an underdeveloped, segregated suburb— and no white person would set foot there. It was too dangerous. If you went there, you were taking a huge risk. Not only was it against the law, but let's just say the people living there would not appreciate you visiting. If you'd told me when I was growing up that we were going to Soweto, I would have said, 'That's where the boogie man lives, and we will be eaten alive.' That is what I thought. That is the message I had received and how I'd processed the information as a child. There was no way of surviving Soweto. So here we are, forty years on from my childhood, a decade after the dismantling of apartheid, and Selma tells me, as casually as anything, that she is taking me to Soweto. I was petrified and, simultaneously, so excited.

I arrived in South Africa early in the morning, and then Selma and I were driving into Soweto. I was almost pinching myself in disbelief. Selma knew her way there like the back of her hand. She drove us straight to where we were going, not in a touristic way, but in the manner of someone who frequents a place with total ease. We were driving to the house of a group of women she had been working with through her political activities. I had no idea what to expect. I was imagining Soweto would now look like a middle-class suburb, because it had been ten years since Mandela had come into power and this was the sort of change I could conceive might have occurred. But I caught a glimpse of Soweto in the distance: bright, bustling, and looking exactly like my idea of a township—shanty houses, cobbled together with wood and corrugated iron. And as I was trying to get my head around this Soweto business, just as we were approaching this shanty town and the fear was really creeping in Selma said—totally out of the blue—'See those street-lights?' I looked up. They were along every street. Nothing out of the ordinary to me. 'Soweto used to have no electricity for its four million people. In my city council days, I rallied hard for it. And we won.'

How can I explain to you what happened to me in that exact moment, when Selma uttered those words and showed me those power lines? I still get goosebumps thinking about it. It's almost impossible to explain exactly why everything turned upside down—or right way up—in that instant. But it did. When Selma told me she was responsible for the electricity in Soweto something happened to me, something clicked. Somehow, she turned the electricity on in my head as well. It was absolutely my call-to-action moment. I can only tell you that I instantly wanted to know what that felt like, to be able to say I'd made a difference to that many people.

To give you a bit of context, the township of Soweto had existed under terrible conditions since it had been created in the 1930s. The problems were innumerable, but in her work around the township Selma had noted the lack of electricity on the streets and found it, to put it mildly, appalling. Without streetlights, Soweto was even more dangerous. It meant crime was rife on the streets, and no one could safely go out after dark. And the homes had no electricity either. Wives were waking up at 2.00 a.m. to iron a shirt with a heated block and light the coal stove to make a cup of tea before their husbands set off to work. People were terribly disadvantaged. If they wanted to study at night, for instance, there was no light for that. When Mandela became friends with Jules, he confessed to him that he'd had no choice but to study by candlelight. This was unthinkable to Selma. There and then she decided to make lighting up Soweto her mission. It was not going to be easy. This was apartheid South Africa; no one cared about that community. But Selma did care and she did not give up. After much struggle, in 1974 she emerged victorious. Electricity came to Soweto. Crime was reduced. The streets were safer. People could read books in their homes. She proved that the government could do better. That we could all do better as citizens. Let there be light!

It was through Selma's action that I realised, *It is possible for me to make a difference.* The action of her being so instrumental to change in that city, and her effect on the lives of millions of people, touched me deeply. It felt like, *Wow, imagine being responsible for that.* My rogue work, rescuing food, surfaced instantly. I didn't have to go looking for a vehicle to make a difference. I already had it in the palm of my hand. I had needed to find a real solution for the food waste in my work life, and I'd found one. But it was in this exact moment that I thought, *I can do this. I can actually do this.* My mind opened to the idea of what it would feel like to feed lots of people. That was the bigger picture. It struck me that there was an opportunity to really, truly make a difference. I intrinsically knew that, somehow, my life would never be the same again.

We arrived at Selma's friend's house and we were greeted by a small group of lovely black ladies in a green-tiled living room. They were all warm and welcoming. It was another world for me, but one that felt so familiar. This was my first experience with black South Africans since my beloved nannies. I had been seventeen when that world had ended for me. It felt like being home and yet also so new and unknown. These women had all been political activists; Selma had been involved with them for years. They started sharing knowledge and information, all as equals, and the whole scene seemed surreal to me. While I was taking all of this in, I was simultaneously in the headspace of, *Oh my God, I'm going to do something, I'm going to help people.* I was reeling. The beauty of this moment just kept unfolding.

When I reflect on the events that followed in my life—creating a food rescue charity—this day had everything to do with it. These beautiful women shifted something inside me. The impact was enormous. Healing is the word that comes to mind, but maybe it's not the right one. It felt as though we were partaking in a new way of living. The nightmare in my head of growing up in South Africa was suddenly being rewired, with this new reality uniting us in such a positive way. The atrocities of apartheid South Africa had changed and were changing through the power of action. Mandela's action. Selma's action. These women's action. Positive action was the purifying force.

When I look back at my formative years in South Africa, even at the hopeful age of seventeen, everything had felt utterly hopeless. It had fleetingly occurred to me to stay and fight the system, but at the time I truly believed things would never change. There were people, like Selma and so many others, however, who did stay, not from apathy or lack of opportunity, but because they believed in showing their support by seeing this through and believing in evolution and revolution. They believed in doing what they could to support South Africa to become what it could and should be. I never thought to give myself that opportunity, even as I became older. Life just continued on, as life does, from one thing to the next. I was born and educated in South Africa, then I left. That was it. And even though I was young, and even though it was barely my choice, I harbour guilt for that. For not standing by my black and brown brothers and sisters who deserved more courage from the privileged few. Fundamentally, I had not known that I could make a difference. But here I was, 33 years later, feeling like maybe I could have. And maybe I could now find a way to make a difference. I could finally find a way to take action, in the country where I lived now. Maybe life was presenting me another chance at courage.

Food is universal. Food equalises us all. Food is about dignity. It is about sharing and caring and love. Food doesn't discriminate. It is for every living being, no matter who you are or the colour of your skin. It is a core, fundamental connector: we all need it. In that sense, my new food rescue idea had everything to do with South Africa. For me it was a way to right a wrong. There is no doubt that I had been carrying a sense of debt, a sense of working towards a redemption from the gross inactivity of my past. And I don't mean to say that there is a link between the atrocities that occurred in South Africa and what we do now in OzHarvest. Nothing can redeem any part of what happened there. And nothing can change the fact that I was not an activist at a time when it really counted. Though I still don't call myself an activist, I knew that day that I wouldn't be able to make a difference on a bigger scale without becoming one.

What an honour it is to be part of something that considers the voiceless, that works to help the dispossessed in our community, that gives a basic sense of dignity and deservedness to many different people. And it's all by virtue of making sure that beautiful quality food reaches every demographic of need. The people who surrounded me growing up—the Florries of my youth—were not given the opportunity to be treated with dignity, were not recognised for their contribution; they were not seen, nor were they heard. Nothing can undo that or what they went through or how we treated them. And although I did not set up OzHarvest to do this in a deliberate sense— it grew from a solution to a problem I had in front of me—it has done this. I dedicate everything good that has come from my work at OzHarvest to Florrie and to all the nameless faces from which I averted my gaze. It is all I can do now.

And it was here, in this green-tiled room in Soweto, that it all solidified. I was going to do this food-waste thing, and do it properly. That night, my adrenalin was pumping. I was plotting and planning and thinking and dreaming. I was so excited. I barely slept for days. I flew back to Australia convinced about starting a food-rescue charity, though it still didn't have a name.

I told absolutely everyone: 'I'm going to start a food-rescue organisation.' I told my family and all the caterers I worked with, and my clients and people in shops and random people on the street. Anyone. I'm doing this. That's it. There was deep intentionality now. Having had the experience of building up my florist shops, of building up RKED, of network marketing: all those experiences taught me that I could make things happen. I had courage. I had strength. I never thought to question whether or not I could start OzHarvest because there was nothing about it, as far as I could see, that might fail. I knew it would be useful, I knew it would be helpful and I knew it would get off the ground and have some kind of importance, because it was important to me. What I have found is that when you follow your instincts you are able to act in a way that you wouldn't normally act. You find capabilities you didn't know were there. You may be shy and suddenly you can speak in public. You may never have seen yourself as a negotiator, and now you are wheeling and dealing. And so, from one day to the next, I was a woman possessed, even without understanding exactly what it was I was getting myself into.

My trip to Soweto had led to an epiphany. I didn't need more stuff, more possessions, more validation, more money. My cup was full. What I desperately wanted was to really feel what it meant to do good. I went from living a totally self-indulgent life with Anton to wanting to live in a way that wasn't just about me and my pleasure. I wanted to serve something bigger than myself. The word 'harvest' started to form in my mind; this was exactly what I had been doing delivering those leftover meals. I was harvesting. I liked it. That's all I had in terms of a vision. I had absolutely no other sense of what needed to happen. But it was something.

This terrifying town from my childhood became my clarion call. In one fated, romantic instant, Soweto undressed herself for me and showed me her humanity—her flesh as my flesh and her blood as my blood. The electricity of Soweto found its way into my body; it lit a thrilling switch and has never stopped lighting my way.

My parents, Abe Hellmann and Sylvia Papilsky, boyfriend and girlfriend during World War II in Cape Town, South Africa, 1940.

*above:* Me at the tender age of one in Johannesburg, 1953.

*left:* My father was an architect in the army and received special dispensation to get married. He was 27 years old and my mother 24 on their glorious wedding day in Queenstown, South Africa, 1941.

Hanging out in the backyard with my sisters and parents.

*above:* My family in 1953 (*clockwise from top left*): me (aged 1), Mum (33), Dad (36), Pam (11) and Margie (6).

*right:* With my sisters on a beachside family holiday in 1955.

*right:* With my mother and father in 1960, shortly after my dad recovered from his crippling car accident. He would let me keep his wooden walking stick by my bed at night for protection as I was afraid of the dark.

*below left:* In my element, competing in the 100-yard race at Sandringham Primary School, Johannesburg.

*below right:* The first time I went to Habonim camp, in 1962. I was happy during the day but cried myself to sleep each night from homesickness!

The woman who would change my life, Selma Browde. She showed me how powerful a woman could be in the world and continues to be a source of awe and inspiration.

Love of my childhood life, Alan Browde, shown here at age eighteen.

My favourite day at King David High School, Johannesburg: Sports Day! I received medals for hurdles, relays and sprinting.

With my cousin Michelle in 1969. I always thought Michelle was beautiful, talented and perfect. She was a real challenge for me during my insecure teen years.

*left:* Des and me at the very beginning of our romance, at Habonim camp, 1969.

*below:* Officially an 'item'.

On the steps of my grandmother's house in 1969, days before I left South Africa forever.

All my love, Ron xxx

*above:* My love letters to Des during our year of separation included photos of me so he wouldn't forget what I looked like!

*left:* New 'pioneers' at Kibbutz Yizre'el in Israel, 1971.

A typical Sabbath afternoon for Des and me included relaxing as one big family by the communal kibbutz swimming pool.

*left:* Neil and Dudi, always clowning around and making us laugh.

Des in the Israeli army in 1971.   Celebrating the end of Des's basic training in the army.

Our kibbutz wedding in 1972, with my body-hugging crocheted dress.

On our European honeymoon, which was cut short by the 1973 Yom Kippur war.

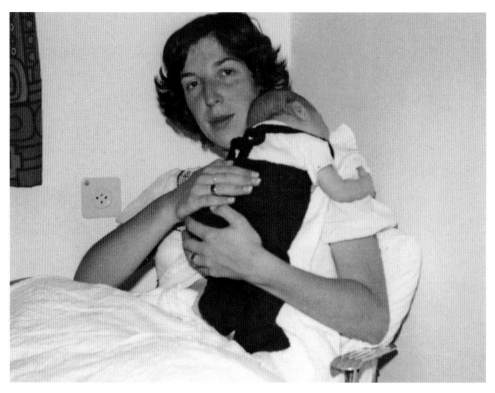

A mother at 22 years of age, with newborn Nadav on the kibbutz in 1974.

Just months after Neil was killed, with baby Nadav and my sister-in-law Jenny in the kibbutz almond orchard.

Happily pregnant with Edo in 1978.

A very proud Nadav bringing
his new baby brother home.

My perm in all its glory! With baby Edo, my sisters Pam and Margie, and nephew Tuval, 1979.

With my babies, Nadav and Edo, in 1979.

Our family of four in our kibbutz backyard.

My sister Pam and I worked together day and night in our Haifa floristry business. Here we are in 1984, decorating one of our many events.

Doing my best to look coordinated at the height of my aerobics obsession in the 1980s.

*right:* New immigrants in Sydney, Australia, 1988.

*below:* Building our dream Australian home in Sydney, 1994, and celebrating in the finished kitchen with teenage Edo and Nadav two years later.

A 1997 corporate event in my prime RKED days.

Principessa Ronni. My fiftieth birthday in 2002, during the decadent Anton era.

Two Jewish mothers on a mission! First trip to India with Ilona Lee and Edo in 2005.

My teacher, Sri Sakthi Narayani Amma.

# CHAPTER 21

# CITY OF AN ANGEL

Whenever I am about to jump into something new in my life, I visit one of my precious sisters—I either hop on a plane to visit Pam in Israel or go to Los Angeles to see Margie. Margie has always been my sounding board. We can talk about anything and everything, and we know how to shop like nobody's business. Sometimes we go straight to the mall from the airport.

Los Angeles also happens to be a city where the event industry excels. Whenever I visited Margie before OzHarvest, I'd always take the time—amidst the sister time—to visit businesses in the event industry to make sure I was ahead of the game, which I almost always felt I was.

At this time, I was a member of the International Special Events Society and one day, shortly after returning from South Africa, I was flipping through their special events directory when my eyes froze on a business called 'Angel Harvest'. There was that word that had been floating around in my head: harvest. Before I'd even read about who they were or what they did, I thought, *Whoa, I love the name of that business! I want to know what kind of events they do.* I presumed it was a regular event company with a great name, since it was advertising in an event company magazine. But then I started reading and saw to my amazement that they rescued leftover food from events. I honestly could not believe it. My heart started beating faster. If I ever needed proof of synchronicity, here it was.

I phoned them immediately, of course, but all I could get was a machine saying, 'If you've got food, leave a message.' Day after day I called them, but could never get through to a real person to tell them: 'Hey, I'm coming all the way from Australia! I want to know how you do what you do.' Obsessed, I rang Margie urgently and said, 'Margie, I'm booking a flight. I'm coming in two days, and you have *got* to find these people for me.' I thought I might land in LA and have to fly out right then and there to meet them somewhere in another state. The listing said they were located in LA, but who knew where the founder was? I was willing to do whatever it took to meet him or her. I thought, *Why would I reinvent the wheel if someone has done it? I've got to learn about this. I want to do it right.* I knew it was what I had to do. There was nothing more to it.

When I arrived at LAX, Margie was there to meet me, and all I said was, 'Did you find the person? Do you have a phone number for me?' Margie looked at me a little shocked and hurt and said, 'Nice to see you, too, and do you think we could go home first?' That's our usual mode—chatting, tea drinking, gossiping, laughing. I said, 'No, Margie. I might have to fly somewhere right now.' I was completely and utterly determined. She was so annoyed, but she said, 'Okay, here's a number I found.' On a little piece of paper, in Margie scribble, was a name—Helen verDuin Palit—and her number. I was practically shaking with anticipation. Margie handed me her big brick cell phone and I called Helen right there, from the arrivals gate.

Well, this woman actually picked up, so I said, 'Hi, I'm Ronni Kahn, I've just landed from Australia, and I'm here because I want to learn about food rescue. I know that I can do this because I know people.' I could see Margie rolling her eyes, dying of embarrassment, but I kept going. 'I can do this,' I said to Helen. 'I'm here to learn because I know I can do this. I know everyone in the event industry in Australia.' We chatted. I finally got off the phone and took one look at Margie's aggrieved face and said, 'What's the matter?' She said, 'You sound like the biggest *schvitzer!*' (That's Yiddish for a jerk or a bragger.) I said, 'But you don't understand, I'm trying to convince her I'm for real, I can do this, I'm not going to waste her time!' I was cringing at my approach after Margie's rebuke, but it didn't seem to have mattered anyway, because despite how I came across, miraculously, Helen said she'd come to Margie's house the very next day to meet up! I was beside myself with excitement. Needless to say, Margie was by no means impressed, but she knew me well enough to know that sometimes I got carried away, to put it mildly.

My capers, however, only seemed to get worse in Margie's eyes. The next day I dressed for the meeting at Margie's house, and I remember my exact outfit. I put on my chocolate-brown barramundi-skin Terry Biviano power stilettos with hot pink soles. And I wore a slinky but corporate-ish dress. I came out of the bedroom and Margie said, 'Oh my gawd, what are you *wearing?*'

'What are you talking about?' I said. 'I have a meeting!'

'Ronni! This woman is going to come in a kaftan and sandals, for God's sake. That's what the charity NGOs wear here in America.

And you're meeting her informally, here at the house! What is your problem?!'

'Margie, I don't care,' I said. 'This is what I wear to meetings, and this is what I'm wearing!'

The doorbell rang and there stood Helen—grey-haired, kaftaned, beaded and sandalled. And there I stood in my full-blown, sexy, stiletto power outfit. Suffice to say, there was not instant rapport. After some terribly fidgety pleasantries, I escaped to make her a cup of tea. Margie had been right. *We are essentially chalk and cheese*, I thought, and the physical difference between us was more than a little awkward. I returned, a little shaky, with her tea, and said nervously, 'I'm not quite sure where to begin.'

'Well, before we start,' she said, 'tell me about those *shoes*!' We broke the ice and we laughed, and we talked about the shoes, and then things got really fun.

Helen had not come from the event industry. Twenty years earlier, she had worked for a not-for-profit that was situated opposite a restaurant. One day, she went in to the restaurant and saw them preparing food in the kitchen and throwing away bucket loads of the insides of potatoes. It was the 1990s, which was the time of the potato-skin appetizer, so she said, 'Can I have the insides?' And they said, 'For God's sake, please, you'll be doing us the biggest favour.' So she began making potato soup for people who needed food, and she realised pretty quickly, if they had potatoes, other places would have other things. And that was what started her off. It was the beginning of the food-rescue organisation in New York named City Harvest, which is now 40 years old. It's enormous. Then she started Angel Harvest in LA, Sunshine Harvest in Miami, Aloha Harvest in Hawaii, and finally Maple Leaf Harvest in Canada. None of them was connected; she'd simply set up each one and moved on to the next. They were each completely independent organisations.

What an impressive woman. She was smart and amazing, and we totally connected. We met up again the next day in her office. She gave me copies of files, forms, templates for everything, which was incredible for me. I used some and didn't use others, but they became my first guides. And then, that was it. I never saw Helen again. I always make sure to honour her for opening her heart and showing me how they rescued food in the United States. I was then able to return to Australia and use the Angel Harvest track record as a base line, creating something that was right for Sydney. Despite having already considered using the word 'harvest', it also felt like a way to honour her role and her incredible work. I still marvel at how that word came and found me. I still marvel that I had the good fortune to meet someone as generous as Helen, my American angel. On the basis of her generosity, and in the model of 'paying it forward', OzHarvest is always committed to sharing its model.

Most of all, however, I will never forget the moment at Margie's house when Helen leaned forward and asked me an important question. It came out of the blue and it took me by surprise. She said, 'Ronni . . . what is your agenda?' I wasn't quite sure what she meant at the time, or what she was getting at, because I thought there was an obvious answer to that question. A little baffled, I simply replied, 'I want to know what it feels like to have done good.' What I didn't know then, but Helen probably knew all too well, were all the distractions that could be found on this trajectory, and the potential to be sidetracked for personal gain. How could I have known this then? But within six months I was on the cover of newspapers and in magazines, and then I understood what Helen already knew. What is your agenda, Ronni? It's a question to keep you in check.

This question is especially useful when I mentor people who come to me to brainstorm ideas of all types. I think in this day and age of social media, people sometimes think charity is a way to become a celebrity. Having this motivation doesn't mean their idea won't be successful. It just means I may not be the most effective mentor for them. But there are also a lot of people who just want to do something good, and they really interest me. They want to become a vessel for something great in the world, and that's a very thrilling thing. They want to give back and do something significant to fulfil something deep within them. I love supporting their growth.

When I started OzHarvest, I had no notion of what being in the charity world would be like. Or that I would be an actual personality inside it. I still don't really understand it. I started OzHarvest because I needed to do it. I had ambition for it, because this job needed to be done, not because I thought I'd have a trajectory that would give me a public profile. On some level, I knew OzHarvest would be big, just because it was a no-brainer—if I have leftover food, other people have leftover food. I knew it would be important. Maybe not right when I started it, but fairly early on. And so the support and the attention has not surprised me. And yet everything has surprised me. All of this—the awards and TV and newspapers and magazines— that wasn't what I ever imagined. I'm still in awe that I've received a single award. I will never get used to that. But that was never my motivation. And I think if my motivation had been different, if I'd wanted fame and acclaim, OzHarvest would be a very different organisation. I don't think it would have the same energy or heart or integrity that it has. And it's those very traits that I think have drawn so many fabulous people to work with OzHarvest.

It's now been seventeen years since Helen asked me that question, and to this day I am still mindful of it and think about it a lot. Every year it means something more to me, and I truly see what an important question she posed. She was calling me to self-examination, to reflection, to accountability within myself. It was a question not just for that moment, but one that would keep revealing itself, one to keep asking myself throughout this journey.

# PART 4

♥

# OZHARVEST

Venice
cable car
speedboat!
Via ferrata ??
Caves
Treetops
Lemons
Gardaland
Gorge Walking
Various Water sports
driving maybe to the alpish part
Ferry

SANPAOLO

# CHAPTER 22

# THE BIRTH OF OZHARVEST

After I came home from LA, the word 'harvest' felt official. I thought, *It's got to be called Australia Harvest*. But somehow that didn't sound quite right. It felt cumbersome. I certainly didn't think my operation would be running all over Australia at that point, but calling it Sydney Harvest sounded so limited. I started brainstorming it with friends, and one day someone said, 'How about Aussie Harvest?' Then it just hit me: OzHarvest. It had a friendly, cheeky kind of ring to me, a *Wizard of Oz* vibe, and I knew I wanted to follow that yellow brick road.

The next step was to register the name and set it up as a company. I knew things would start feeling a bit more real when I did that. I didn't know who to turn to initially, but then I remembered Harland Koops, a top-tier lawyer who had taken on a little case I'd had at RKED years before. It had been a teeny case for him, but I imagine it may have been a welcome relief from his huge billion-dollar cases.

It had been a very big case for me, however, and he'd saved me from something that could have been really messy. He'd recognised I was a little business being screwed over by a large company. It tapped into something within him. He was so helpful. And he was also excellent, and we won.

I called him and said, 'I'd love to come see you, Harland, it's another kind of left-of-field thing.' I'm sure he thought, *She's got another quick, quirky little case. Great!*

'Sure! Come in!' he said. I arrived at this meeting, and he had five of his associates sitting there with him in their big boardroom.

'Oh, okay,' I said, 'this is a little intense.'

And he said, 'Well, you bring us interesting cases. We're all ears.'

'Wait till you hear this one,' I said. 'It's very interesting because in this one, there is no money involved whatsoever!' I then told them what I wanted to do.

They just loved it and said, 'We're going to help you.' So Harland and his team set everything up, and OzHarvest officially became a registered company.

About a minute after registering the OzHarvest name, I realised that I was going to need some money. I was still working at RKED, and my sons and I were delivering leftover food unofficially to shelters in my RKED business van, late at night after all my events. That was it. But I wanted to pick up food from other caterers, other places, anyone who had good leftover food. For that, I would need a separate van with refrigeration, a driver, lots of fuel, an office space and someone to answer the phone and run logistics. I was still running my business full time, so it wasn't as if my RKED van and I were available to do all that. At the time, my brother-in-law, Anthony

Kahn (Des's brother), worked for Macquarie Bank, one of Australia's large financial institutions, which was incredibly fortuitous for me. I went to speak to him about OzHarvest: about what I wanted to do and where and how to get funding. And he immediately said, 'Ronni, go and see the Macquarie Foundation.'

It was the early days of the Macquarie Foundation but they were ahead of the curve. They were investing in social entrepreneurs and social businesses. These were foreign concepts to me. I'd never even heard the words. I didn't know my food-rescue idea fitted into this model or framework. I said to Anthony, 'Sure, I'll go. But what should I say to them?' And he said, 'Just tell them what you've told me.'

He arranged an introduction, though I hadn't a clue what I was going to say. I had no idea because I'd never asked for funding for anything. I'm such a non-planner on so many levels in my life, for better or for worse. I didn't jot anything down on a piece of paper, I didn't have a written plan of any kind. I simply thought, *All I want is fifty thousand dollars*. I walked in to the meeting and met a woman called Julie White. She was the head of the foundation at the time, and she instantly seemed impressive and incredibly intimidating. It was just the two of us in a big boardroom, and I said, 'Hi, my name is Ronni Kahn. I'm going to start a food-rescue organisation and I need some seed funding.'

'Tell me more,' she said.

'Well,' I said, 'it's been done in the United States, so I know it's possible. And from my industry experience in event management, I *know* there is leftover food here in Sydney, every day, in lots of places. And I *know* there are people in need, and I want to connect those two.' It hadn't occurred to me to prepare more than that, but there was really nothing more to it, in my mind. That was it, that was my spiel.

And she said, 'That is a brilliant idea.' And then she said, 'So, how are you going to do it?'

'I'm going to get a vehicle, I'm going to get an office space, and I'm going to talk to all the people I know, because I already know so many people who have surplus food. I'm just going to connect the people I know with those who need food, because I also know there are a lot of them. I don't know how many there are, but I know there are some.' I hadn't done any research about food vulnerability. I didn't go in there and say, 'There are two million people in Australia who need food.' I hadn't considered doing any of that! But what I had done, throughout my event life, was sell dreams. That is what I'd spent my life doing in my RKED business. I knew about that.

In my event business I'd simply walk into a room and someone would say, 'What are you going to do for us?'

And I would say, 'I'm going to give you the most spectacular night of your life.'

'How?' they'd reply.

And I'd say, 'It's going to look like fairy land, feel like fairy land, and people are going to experience your magic.'

'What does that really mean?' they'd ask.

So I'd say, 'Well, I could show you, and you could pay me to do a show and tell, and then you will need to pay me again to do the real thing. *Or* you can choose to believe me.' And everyone chose to believe me. So it simply didn't occur to me that this woman wouldn't believe me. And she did believe me!

I walked out of the meeting and immediately called Anthony, and then called everybody else and said, 'Oh my God, it went so well, it's brilliant, it's fantastic, it was amazing, and they are going to give us the money! She is going to fund me!'

'That's amazing!' said Anthony. He went back to Julie and said, 'It's fantastic that you're going to fund Ronni's new food rescue organisation.'

'What?!' she replied. 'I never said I would!' Then she called me and asked, 'Why are you telling people that I'm going to fund you?'

'Because you told me it was a brilliant idea and that you could see its value. And you asked me such great questions and I answered all your great questions,' I said.

'Ronni, I never told you that I would give you the money. I told you it was a great idea. You can't tell people that I'm giving you money if I haven't told you that I'm giving you money. There's a lot more to it, you know. It's a little more involved than you think.'

A bit sheepishly, I said, 'Oh, okay.'

It was true. I realised she hadn't *really* committed to anything when I walked out the door. But that's not what I had chosen to hear. When she said that it was such a brilliant idea, I heard that she was absolutely going to fund it. It's embarrassing now that I got it so wrong. But I was on such a roll, such a high about what I was going to do, that I forgot to be embarrassed at the time. I'd gone to South Africa, I'd seen what Selma had done, and I had Soweto inside me, so I just knew I could do this. Failure never crossed my mind. I was following something that seemed so sensible, so right. And I was following this wonderful feeling of excitement. It was fuelling everything. *In any case*, I thought, *funding or no funding, I'm doing it myself already, so no one can really tell me otherwise.* So technically, failure was impossible.

I don't think Julie had come across someone quite like me actually. I think she thought I had all this crazy *chutzpah* (the Yiddish word for audacity and cheek). But in fact, the confidence wasn't in me or my ability, it was in my core belief that leftover food should feed people and not go to waste. I felt you would have to be insane to say no to this idea.

She called me a few days later and said, 'Ronni, I'm calling to tell you that I am going to give you the money.'

'Thanks, Julie,' I said. 'I told you so.'

# CHAPTER 23

# BROOM CLOSET OFFICE

Very quickly I realised that whatever I could get for free, I should. Fifty thousand dollars had seemed like a lot of money, but once you hire your first staff member for a year, it's suddenly not so much. I needed office space, desperately. I didn't want to run the charity out of RKED. I knew it wouldn't be good to mix the two. I wanted OzHarvest to be independent, though close to RKED, so I could run back and forth when I needed to, because I thought I might need to do that quite a lot.

I was essentially running two full-time business—RKED and OzHarvest. It got weird actually. Funny weird. I'd be discussing the intricacies of a five-course menu to a very fancy client, while at the same time imagining how I'd manage the leftovers, because I knew that no matter how hard I tried there always would be some. It felt a bit like having a split personality! Or like I was playing Robin Hood. It was an unexpected, thrilling juggle. It was never part of my plan to give up my event business. It wasn't like this whole food-rescue thing was going to take over my life, was it?

The next big meeting that Julie arranged was with a new partner of their business, Greg Goodman. Goodman Group specialises in industrial sites, and that was pretty lucky, because that was exactly what I needed. I was invited to a meeting in a big boardroom at the Goodman offices. I walked in with a single intention: to be given an office space near RKED. There were twelve grey-suited men around an oval table, all with their arms folded. I walked in and said, 'Hi! My name is Ronni Kahn and I'm here to tell you that I'm going to start a food-rescue organisation.'

'Hang on, stop,' said Greg. 'What do you want?'

I said, 'My business is on Mitchell Road in Alexandria, and I don't think the charity should run out of my office. So I need a little office space, and I'd really like one close to Mitchell Road, so it will be convenient for me to run my business and oversee this charity at the same time.'

'Okay,' he said.

And I said, 'Oh, okay.'

Then he said, 'What else do you want?' I was seriously unprepared for any other questions. But I knew we needed a van.

'Well,' I said, 'I'm going to need a van so we can rescue the food and deliver it.'

'Okay, I'll give you a van. What else do you need?' he asked.

I was doubly unprepared for this. I had to think quickly. 'Umm, two vans?' I said in a high-pitched squeak.

'Okay,' he said.

I was so shocked at this point that before anyone had time to change their minds I said, 'Okay, I'm outta here! Thank you. Bye!'

Our new office was triangular, the size of a large broom closet, and was located in the storeroom of a café. I used to say, 'My laptop really is on my lap!' The space simply had a small desk and a phone, but it was exactly what we needed. So now I had an office, two vans, money to hire a couple of part-time drivers and an office administrator, and I had all the leftover food from RKED events to give to a few charities. I'd just spoken to my local health-food store, which was also keen to donate any leftovers it had. And then a caterer who had surplus food got on board, who knew another caterer who had food, who knew another caterer who had food, and the food supply started snowballing.

It turned out a lot of people had exactly the same problem I did. Beautiful, untouched food was going straight into the trash, and none of us had thought there was another alternative.

Then one day, Anthony called me and said, 'I need you to meet someone. Her name is Elaine Booth. She's just arrived from the UK. Her husband works for Macquarie Bank and travels a lot, and she doesn't work and barely knows anyone in Sydney. She may be keen to volunteer, to support you in some way. And you could be doing her a *mitzvah* (Yiddish for good deed) because she's bored out of her skull at the moment.'

I met with Elaine, and instantly I could tell she was brilliant, with an IQ of a million. At the end of the meeting, she said to me, 'I think I can do one day a week.' I'm pretty sure she thought she'd be answering a few phone calls when they came through. Little did she know that her intentions of 'helping out' would take the dramatic turn of completely 'setting up' OzHarvest!

Two months later, Elaine was volunteering for us six days a week. I don't think she knew what had hit her. She fell for us hook, line and sinker! I was still full time at RKED, as well as securing OzHarvest funding and procuring donations such as desks, photocopiers, computers, fridges and so forth. Elaine set up every bit of the office infrastructure. Within five minutes she was out buying our first vans, arranging refrigeration, hiring drivers, sorting out all the logistics. She had to work out matters such as how to get a van from A to B across the city in nose-to-tail traffic and no parking, or where to take half a ton of fresh food that's suddenly been donated late on a Friday night. She was on the phone nonstop, broadening our network, calling food outlets, finding out if they had food left over that they might want to donate. Nobody knew us. We had to spread the word and explain what we did. She also had to call all the existing charities that fed people, give them our spiel and ask, 'How can we help you? What do you need?'

I remember Elaine saying, 'Ronni, all anyone wants to know is, "What's the catch? How much is this going to cost us?"' No one could get their head around the fact that this beautiful food was going to be genuinely free, and that OzHarvest would deliver it directly to them. Elaine had to reassure the agencies that we didn't want anything from them other than their satisfaction! They were also concerned that we would not arrive when we said we would, which would throw their preparation and schedules completely out of whack. She established many relationships with amazing people who were doing their best to help others, with very slim resources. She had to lay the foundations of trust, so they could rest assured that we were reliable and professional.

A few times when Elaine went to meetings at shelters, she was literally crunching used needles underfoot. The juxtaposition of the different sides of her life was not lost on her. She was out of her comfort zone in many ways, but was also happy and fulfilled to be with us. She was my very first volunteer, which was momentous in itself, but in addition I couldn't have asked for anyone more incredible. She was and is a wonderful, capable and talented human being, who has left a real legacy at OzHarvest, and in our society at large.

Around this time one of Macquarie's people, Jane Rotsey, recognised that there was power in the story of a founder, and she loved my story and the notion that food was being rescued. She started getting the word out about OzHarvest and started pitching it to media. It wasn't long before I did my first radio interview, and suddenly more volunteers started lining up. Elaine and I would send them walking around the busy city streets, speaking to food businesses and telling them, 'There's this new charity, and you can give them your leftover food so it doesn't have to go in the bin.' People were really into it. Everyone can connect with the idea that food should not go to waste, and that there is something inherently obscene about throwing away good, unused food.

Before long, we began to have a track record under our belt. Food was being rescued and delivered, and we were ready to launch OzHarvest officially, to open our doors and make this thing real. In November 2004, I crammed ten people into our closet-sized office space and ceremoniously opened OzHarvest. I made a speech. I cried. We cheered, and we've never looked back. To this day, I can picture the space and the people. It felt totally surreal and yet it made all the sense in the world.

Elaine volunteered with us full time for three years, until she and her husband returned to the UK. Funnily enough, I've never seen Greg Goodman in person since that day in the boardroom, but I have the privilege of working with Jo Cameron (my 'sister from another mister') and her wonderful team at the Goodman Group on an ongoing basis. Greg Goodman has given us millions of dollars and continues to support us significantly. His name is 'good-man'. No coincidence. What a name. What a good man he is.

# CHAPTER 24

# THE POWER OF A POINT

Julie from Macquarie really was utterly terrifying to me. She was one tough cookie, to put it mildly. I can say she was terrifying with no qualms, because I think she both knew it and prided herself on it; she felt it would bring out the best in her people. She put a sense of rigour and stamina into the Macquarie Foundation, which continues to have an extraordinary reputation to this day. I have no doubt that this is, at least in part, due to her leadership. She is so dedicated. But she also had this way about her that could easily have people in tears. I'd been warned, so I trod lightly. Nevertheless, I was petrified.

One day, shortly after she agreed to fund OzHarvest, Julie invited me to do a presentation for her team. This was my first OzHarvest presentation. I stood up in front of about fifty people and presented quite simply and earnestly what I was going to do with my food-rescue business. I imagine it was short and sweet; maybe a little clumsy, but from the heart. Then right at the very end of my talk—in front of everybody—she said, 'This is absolutely not good enough!

You have to have a PowerPoint. Go away and do it again, next time with PowerPoint.'

I went home a little crestfallen, then ran straight to Colin, my right-hand man at RKED. Since that first job at Star City, Colin had been working with me, for ten years by this time. We'd become family to each other. I'd sell a dream to clients, busying myself creating and having fun ideas, then he'd go out and bring all of it to life. He couldn't drum up the business himself, but he could get stuff done. He supported everything I did, and was core to RKED.

Colin had already helped me create the first OzHarvest flyer. He could see I was doing less and less RKED work and becoming more and more immersed in OzHarvest, and I think he was pretty much freaking out. But this didn't stop him from being totally supportive. So I said, 'Colin, please help me.' I was in serious PowerPoint need and, as usual, he found a way and saved the day. Within hours, I had an impressive PowerPoint presentation and was Julie-ready.

For the next presentation, I was there, ready with PowerPoint, and the slideshow itself was good enough, but my operation of it was not exactly up to speed. I was talking and simultaneously futzing around with the clicker thing, and the PowerPoint presentation was really in the way. And it was so boring! It was slowing me down and getting in the way of my flow. It was so bad that halfway through my talk, Julie yelled out, 'Ditch the PowerPoint! You absolutely have no idea how to use PowerPoint!' In that moment, when Julie publicly shamed me for the second time, something quite magical happened. In that fated instant, I became free, forever, of PowerPoint. Through Julie's realisation that PowerPoint wasn't right for me—and that I was, quite probably, untrainable in PowerPoint—she utterly freed me to be able to say 'I don't do PowerPoint' forever more. That was my first and last PowerPoint presentation, and I've been freewheeling ever since. Hanging loose and loud and proud of my PowerPoint-less presentations, every which way I go, all over the world.

These days people live and die by PowerPoint. Even first-grade kids are asked to present projects in PowerPoint. But, as God is my witness, I am living proof that you can build a whole organisation *without* PowerPoint. To this day, I will not go there, and I'm thankful to Julie for giving me licence to never use PowerPoint again. It's not because I was scared off, because of course I could pick it up and learn how to use it if I wanted to do so. Rather, it's because, in that moment, I realised that I like to talk from my heart. I don't always know what I am going to say, but this keeps things fluid and fresh. Talking from the heart is something I feel proud of doing. There is enough power and enough of a point in that, I'm certain of it.

Of course, I am aware that people like to say 'three million meals have been delivered' and then have a PowerPoint that says, 'three million meals have been delivered'. They like to emphasise what they are saying. I'm sure there is some science around this, about how our brains register things, so I'm sure I'm missing something, but apart from having a special diagram or something imperative to look at or watch, it seems completely pointless to me, if you'll pardon the pun. Personally, I am always disappointed when there is a PowerPoint component, even in a TED talk. I'm sure it helps the speaker feel they've done their homework. I'm sure it seems prepared and professional, and makes the information feel more official and legitimate. But above all, from my experience, it works to disconnect the audience from the speaker. And maybe it's done because intimacy is hard, especially in corporate environments.

When I speak at lectures, or wherever I may be, and the sound guy asks, 'Where is your PowerPoint?' I say, 'Oh, didn't anyone tell you? I don't do PowerPoint,' and he often becomes nervous and says something like, 'Oh, so, so, so . . . should we just have your name up on the screen?' And I say, 'Sure, that's fine. Go ahead and just have my name up.' God forbid, people should actually stare at me for an hour! Honestly, PowerPoint seems to run on the premise that staring at a person speaking and processing what they are saying, live, is essentially terribly hard or boring or nerve-racking for the audience and/or for the speaker. And yet it's through this whole PowerPoint fiasco that I've discovered one of my big skills in life: when I talk, I engage from the heart, and people often appear to be riveted. Maybe having nothing but me up there has forced me (and them) to be more present.

If PowerPoint works for you, more power to you. But I say and will continue to say, *Less PowerPoint, more power.*

# CHAPTER 25

# THE LUNCH MEETING

So much of my education came from the Macquarie Foundation. They were serious about investing in social entrepreneurs. There were lots of us. And they didn't just invest with their money. They'd find guest speakers and have training sessions, and really educate us in invaluable ways. I was invited to participate in many different events and experiences that helped improve my skill set, and it felt amazing. Weeks after receiving my very first seed money from them, Julie arranged an important meeting for OzHarvest, for more fundraising opportunities. She said I was to meet two women from a Melbourne foundation who were quite powerful in terms of giving away money. They were coming to Sydney to meet people; little did I know that this lunch would end up being one of the biggest learning curves of my career.

It was at the Museum of Sydney. I'd never been there to eat before, and when I arrived, I could see it was a very fancy lunch. In the event sector, we didn't go out to fancy lunches with clients. I'd often meet clients at their homes, where I'd look around their house, learn about them, tell them how I could best reflect their lives in their event. So this fancy lunch date to discuss business was a pretty new idea to me. And my understanding was, people are very, very busy, so above all, don't waste their precious time. I wanted to be effective and respectful. I decided beforehand that I *wasn't* going to eat lunch, because I wouldn't be able to eat and talk at the same time, plus this would make it a swift meeting for them.

The women arrived, dressed to the nines. 'Are you going to eat anything?' they asked.

'Oh no, I don't eat over lunch meetings.'

They looked at each other. 'Oh. Okay, well . . . we're eating.'

'Okay, sure,' I said. 'I can just talk while you eat.'

'Would you like a glass of wine?' they asked.

'Oh, no, I don't drink at lunchtime.'

They looked at each other again. 'Oh, okay, well . . . would you like a cup of tea?'

I said, 'No, no, a glass of water will do me just fine.' They looked at each other yet again.

Their food arrived, and they proceeded to eat their lunch. They ate while I talked and talked and watched, and slowly died of starvation. Two minutes after I finished giving my spiel, they just started chatting amongst themselves about other things, completely uninterested in anything I had just said. And I continued to sit there and watch them, while I sipped my water. It was the most terrible, awkward meeting of my life and, obviously, there was zero connection. I was mortified by the end of that lunch. There was nothing left to do but excuse myself. Thank God I left before dessert! I was weak at the knees from hunger, but I had thought that my approach was the right thing to do. Needless to say, I never received a single dollar from them. The whole thing had been singularly unsuccessful.

When I told Julie that the meeting didn't go at all well, she said, 'Oh dear, you'd better meet my friend Kitty Hilton. She might be able to help you, though I'm not sure you're helpable!' I think I was a real challenge to the foundation. They believed in the OzHarvest cause, and Julie must have believed in me personally, but most people in their program knew so much about philanthropy, and I was not one of those people. I was running things in my own, intuitive way. My way of doing things was, mostly, getting results, yet it baffled them.

Luckily, Kitty was a fundraising guru. We met up and we sat down, and I told her everything about the lunch meeting. 'Oh, God, Kitty,' I said, 'I don't know why, but that was the worst meeting I've had in my entire life. They sat and ate and drank wine while I spoke! Can you believe it?'

She said, 'Uh, yes, Ronni. That's what people do at a lunch meeting. That's why it's called a "lunch meeting". Fundraising is relationship-building. People give money to people they like. If somebody eats, you eat. If somebody leans over, you lean over. And if they drink wine, you drink wine.'

Well, I was blown away but I took on that lesson quick smart. Kitty taught me that while the cause is always important, it's really about being able to relate to the person in front of you, and this has stood me in good stead ever since. People think there is an art to fundraising, but ultimately, it's about connection and authenticity, and finding the humanity in each other. It can be quite beautiful. It can be a delightful opportunity, whether you get the money or not.

It turns out I was, in fact, helpable. Since that undignified lunch, I've shared many cups of tea, glasses of wine, desserts, meals, and even tears, at many meetings. And the Macquarie Foundation invested in OzHarvest for a full ten years, even though they generally only fund for a maximum of three years. It was an amazing relationship and I learnt so much. I am eternally grateful to my brother-in-law Anthony, as well as Julie, Jane, Kitty, and the whole Macquarie Foundation, for watering the seeds of an OzHarvest in the making.

# CHAPTER 26

# REPAIRING THE WORLD

My new food rescue work brought lots of opportunities. One of the skills I needed to cultivate was speaking in public, because I was being invited to share the story of founding OzHarvest to businesses and social groups on a regular basis. Aside from the little pep talks I'd given in my network marketing days, I hadn't done any public speaking. It was exciting but a huge leap.

When I was fifteen years old, the headmaster of my high school encouraged me to consider running for school captain. The catch was that in order to be considered, I had to give a speech at school assembly. After I got over the shock that he even thought I was capable of being school captain, I said no, because I felt I could never give a speech to 800 people, or to any people. I chose not to do it; it was just too terrifying. That kind of thing was for special people and, at the time, I didn't feel there was a special bone in my body. But when I was fifty-one, I stood up in front of a group of strangers and gave my first public presentation. It was a simple, short talk that took place in a regular Sydney office on a regular workday, but it was deeply significant to me. It was the first time I'd had something to say that felt meaningful and that was my own. The things I wanted to say felt bigger than my terror. It's hard to believe that these days, talking and sharing in public are what I love most about my job. They are how I connect to people from the heart. My fifteen-year-old self is still completely incredulous.

As the public speaking part of my life took off, the impact of what I was saying and sharing became really important to me, beyond the fact of having started OzHarvest. I was trying to make sense of what I was doing beyond rescuing food. I knew there was more at work here. Strangely, what came flooding back to me as a kind of rudder on this very new ship in this very new sea were the lessons I'd received at Habonim—my childhood Jewish Youth Movement— more than 40 years earlier. In particular, the idea of *tikkun olam* (repairing the world) came sweeping back into my consciousness. A concept that had felt so unattainable in apartheid South Africa was now within the realms of possibility. I felt that the underlying purpose of OzHarvest was to right a wrong: the wrong being throwing away food, the right being placing it in the hands of those who needed it, ensuring resources for vulnerable people in our community and fulfilling a moral duty. *Tikkun olam* was starting to make perfect sense to me.

What I learnt over the years from different books and teachers was that *tikkun olam* was never only applicable to social activism. It goes without saying that we will all hopefully choose to do our bit when there is an injustice in front of us: this is so important.

The early days of OzHarvest. Handing out rescued food to a grateful staff member at a homeless shelter in 2004.

My first OzHarvest van, donated by Macquarie Goodman.

Rescuing food from Sydney's iconic Harry's Café de Wheels in 2005.

Outside Parliament House in Canberra, having just been presented with the Australian Local Hero of the Year award in 2010.

At our 2012 CEOCookOff with beloved chef Maggie Beer.

The 2014 CEOCookOff with chef Neil Perry (*left*) and Qantas CEO Alan Joyce (*right*).

At OzHarvest headquarters in Sydney, about to load crates of beautiful rescued food into our vans to be delivered to shelters.

My new silver hair at OzHarvest headquarters in 2016.

Our newly branded food rescue trucks, collecting and delivering food all over Australia.

Photo by Penny Bradfield

Sealing a 2015 tri-partisan agreement to halve food waste in Australia by 2025, with (*left to right*) Shadow Minister for the Environment Mark Butler, Greens Representative Larissa Waters and Minister for the Environment Greg Hunt.

Photo by Nikki To

The 2016 CEOCookOff with (*left to right*) Richard Deutsch (then Chairman of OzHarvest) and participating chefs Neil Perry and Matt Moran.

HRH Camilla, Duchess of Cornwall, honouring us with a 2016 visit to the OzHarvest headquarters.

OUR PURPOSE IS TO NOURISH OUR COUNTRY

Alan Browde visiting from South Africa in preparation for the launch of South Africa Harvest in 2016. Establishing SAHarvest is one of the most fulfilling experiences I have had to date.

Visiting Selma Browde in South Africa, 2017.

Soweto, forever in my heart.

Launching UKHarvest with Jamie Oliver at the first London CEOCookOff in 2017.

There are always beautiful moments at the Nourish graduation.

The welcoming 'open heart' doors of our OzHarvest Market, the first free supermarket in Australia.

Inside the waste-free OzHarvest Market.

Making a giant paella at the 2018 CEOCookOff with team PwC, headed by chef Miguel Maestre.

High on love at the 2019 CEOCookOff.

Taste-testing wasted produce on a Queensland farm while filming the documentary *Food Fighter* in 2016.

Behind the scenes of *Food Fighter*, at a landfill site in Thailand.

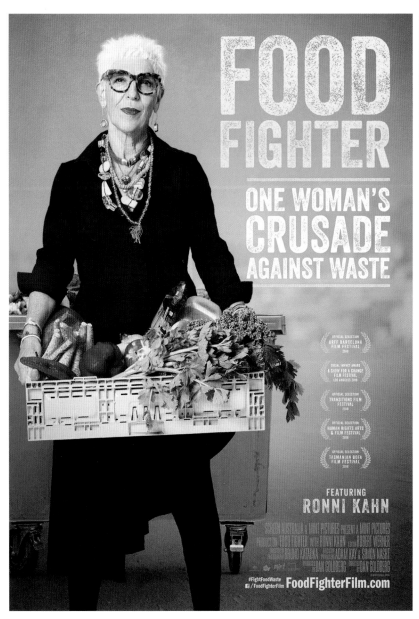

When director Dan Rosenberg approached me about making a film, I thought it was going to be about food waste exclusively. To my surprise, he decided that the documentary needed a protagonist: me! The crew followed me for a couple of years and it became an intimate journey, documenting my attempt to make peace with my past by opening South Africa Harvest, as well as UKHarvest. It was such a special time. This is the poster that appeared outside cinemas around Australia when *Food Fighter* was released in 2018.

World Environment Day at Sydney's Martin Place, 2019.

Hosting a sustainable rescued dinner at OzHarvest headquarters with chef
Massimo Bottura at the helm.

Spending a magical afternoon with my wise and extraordinary friend Major Hilton Harmer.

Overjoyed at OzHarvest's fifteenth birthday celebration in 2019.

My family (*left to right*): Jasmine, Emily, baby Lalita, cows Shambo and Rumi, Edo, Lev, me, Beau, Jessy and Nadav.

Jessy and me in India, during the final stages of writing this book.

But *tikkun olam* is a subtler process. It can be a way of life. It is the slow, precise, modest practice of living our lives with awareness and harmony. It is an intention. These efforts, no matter where you live, or how personal or how seemingly small they are, can be the ones that change the world. And when I say 'change the world', I really mean that every single act we participate in reverberates. Everything is connected. If we intentionally consider our next-door neighbour today, or feed and bathe our kids, or feed ourselves nourishing food, we are, hands down, participating in life-giving acts that bring harmony, in one way or another, to everything. This is how we repair the world.

I like to think that any time we do something in the name of goodness, every time we do something that follows our most simple truth, it affects everything around us. It's in the way we treat our children; it's in the way we treat the bus driver when she or he takes us to work in the morning; it's in the way we treat our co-workers. It's in the way we run our businesses and the way we choose to think about our employees. It is an accepted idea that our business is there so we can make money. But couldn't we do the same business with the intention of making money *and* making it a vehicle for good? This is possible in so many ways.

It doesn't matter what your role is or what level you are at. You don't have to wait until you are promoted or until you are the boss. You are the one who knows about your work. Who would be better equipped than you to know what needs to be done, changed, tweaked, created? Trust your observations, your experience. When corporations ask me to inspire their staff, or when people I talk to want something that I seem to have, I say, 'Start exactly where you are.' This is how OzHarvest began. It began with my observation, my lived experience of knowing my work from the inside. It began with a simple intention of doing something good.

Whether you are a child, or a student, or an artist or a business-woman, or an activist or a stay-at-home dad or an accountant or a retired person—we can all be involved in *tikkun olam*. It recognises that we are each part of a collective, and that we each have the ability to bring harmony, through our actions, through our work and in our togetherness in big and small ways—though really that means in recognised and not recognised ways, because it's all big. *Tikkun olam* is such an exciting idea and it really inspires me. Changing one thing in someone's life completely motivates me. And that change in turn changes me in new, surprising ways. It's one of my favourite parts about my work *and* about life, hands down. It's so powerful. And I hope that OzHarvest is a beacon for that mindset. The mindset of consciously participating, on a daily basis, in bringing peace and harmony to ourselves and others, in whatever way we can. Through this process, we continue to perfect our world. This is our natural process as human beings. *Tikkun olam* is that evolution.

Once, I heard something beautiful—I don't remember where and I don't remember when (probably from a rabbi)—but it was along these lines. There are two ways of viewing the world. We can see it as broken, and from that view it needs the rather urgent work of repair. Or we can view the world as perfect in its imperfection, so it doesn't need repair but rather participation through living and playing a role in that balance. The catch is that perfection is often hidden. Perfection is hard for us to see as humans. At first glance, our many societies and our planet look to be a mess in so many ways.

But what's so beautiful is that by participating in restoring the balance, as though by some alchemical miracle, our eyes begin to perceive the perfection of the world in all its glory. It changes us and it changes the world naturally. Harmony happens naturally. *Tikkun olam* is about participating in that state of harmony.

# CHAPTER 27

# AMMA

I was born Jewish, but there wasn't a skerrick of spirituality in the Judaism I grew up with. There was nothing that moved my heart in any way, no synagogue service with any personal meaning to me, no ritual I ever understood. The whole thing appeared to me as a rite we all went through. A tradition. A culture. Nothing ever penetrated me on a soul level. I also skipped the hippie movement of the 1960s, and all the flower power. I was living on the kibbutz at the time and, as a young mother, was completely oblivious to the mind-altering substances that were being used, that were taking people on spiritual journeys. When I finally found yoga in the 1980s, it was simply great exercise.

In 2004, one month after officially opening the doors of OzHarvest, one of my son Edo's closest friends invited him to visit a spiritual teacher in a tiny rural village in the south of India. The offer to go to India to meet a spiritual master captivated Edo immediately. At 26, it was the perfect time for him to explore his inner life, and off he went. Pretty soon he was calling to tell me what was going on, and he sounded like a completely different person. He was emotional, he was full of joy, and this had all happened in just a couple of weeks. He told me he'd met someone who had changed his life, someone who was giving him new meaning. And it wasn't a girl! It was a guy, and he was calling this man his guru. This was intriguing to me, but totally foreign. I had no idea what to make of it. I phoned Des immediately. Whenever anything happens with our kids, we connect straight away. 'Do you think our son has totally lost it?'

'Sure sounds like it,' he retorted. Ilona, the mother of Edo's friend was as lost as I was. There was only one thing that two Jewish mothers like us could do: get on a plane and rescue our children from what was probably a very dangerous cult.

Once we arrived in India, we needed to be driven for three hours to reach the tiny village, along the most shambolic, broken roads we'd ever seen in our lives. I'm not even sure you could call them roads. We were dodging cows, trucks, carts of hay, motorbikes with whole families on the back. And absolutely *everyone* was blasting their horns. Meanwhile, Ilona and I were in the back seat of a very old car, holding on for dear life with our eyes closed, not sure we'd even make it. I couldn't believe that all this screeching would lead us to a meditative place. We had no sense of what we were getting ourselves into or what demands—if any—would be made of us. We had no reference point. All we knew was that there was a temple, and we knew there would be an Indian guy teaching stuff. Mainly, we knew that our children were there. And we knew we were in for an adventure.

We arrived on New Year's Eve and were taken straight to our boys, who we were surprised to see were wearing skirts. It turns out they were Indian dhotis, traditional men's attire. They were there with about 50 other visiting Westerners, all dressed in Indian garb. Edo was radiant, and the excitement was palpable, because everyone was gathered waiting for this guru they called Sri Sakthi Narayani Amma. There was such a vibe that night. There were people from all corners of the globe, and I was in and out of conversations about gods and goddesses and healing and philosophy. And there was exotic live music going on—drums and harmoniums and bells and a type of Indian saxophone. It was ashram jazz! I was completely transported to another world. All the priests were wearing oranges and yellows, and it was just like all the Bollywood films I'd seen. It felt exotic, and it didn't take long for Ilona and me to feel quite caught up in the 'cult' ourselves. And then, everything stood still somehow. Amma had arrived . . .

When Amma walked in, I just felt, *This is an extraordinary human.* I didn't know why, I didn't know how, but it was a profound feeling. Amma proceeded to give a short discourse—like a little teaching or sermon—and this would happen often throughout the time we stayed. We all sat around and listened with utmost attentiveness. You could hear a pin drop. And it was in these short talks that I really started hearing the whole notion of purpose. I'd heard the idea of purpose before, especially through my network marketing days, but I hadn't thought about what it would feel like to see the work you do as something sacred, something that is for the world, and to feel destined to do it. I heard Amma talk about 'doing good', and I heard him say, 'Feeding people is a precious deed', and 'Service is the purpose of living'. It was all about good actions and kindness, and it was at the level of the everyday. It was about right here, right now, with the people who are sitting next to you. It felt like my heart and my head were connecting. It felt heart-expanding. There was no judgement. There was only acceptance of who you were. The teaching was focused not on what you could get for yourself but rather how you could be of service in any given situation. And in light of all this, ironically, I started understanding what Judaism was about. I had been steeped in Judaic culture but disconnected from its spiritual core. I saw that, essentially, Judaism is a religion of practice, not theology. The whole idea of a *mitzvah*, in a nutshell, is the obligation to participate in good deeds.

I remember asking my first question at one of these talks. 'How can people find their true calling?' I asked.

And Amma said this: 'People are always saying, "What I want to do is this, what I want to do is that." It's always about what they *want* to do. They wait and wait and wait for when the time comes that they can do what they want to do. But the real question to ask is not what do I want to do but what does the world need from me? This will require your heart, not necessarily your education. The heart is where this question and this answer lives. Once you follow that direction, life opens up so many possibilities to you that will bring you true joy. Once you begin playing in that field, you realise you can create whatever you want. So be of service. Ask the question, "What does the world need from me?" It is the path to true happiness.'

The next morning, I was standing in the temple when Amma walked past, and I just crumpled to the floor. I literally fell, in a sort of slow motion, delicately, like a broken flower. I still can't explain exactly what happened. But I can say that I have never felt that kind of energy, in the same way, at any other time in my life. There was no returning from that moment, for me. It was my first experience of true soul connection. I was a goner.

What I came to witness, over the next few weeks, was that this man spent the entirety of his days steeped in ritual. The intention of these ancient rituals was to bring peace and harmony to the world. But more impressively, he had created the most awe-inspiring social projects in this tiny rural village. From a state-of-the art hospital, to incredible bilingual schools for the local children, to environmental programs, afforestation programs, midwifery programs: the list went on and on. It was undeniable that there was vision here, and it was inspired and life-giving and uplifting to witness. The possibilities were endless. Nothing was ever enough. The service to this community and the world at large kept going and going.

One day during my two-week visit, I happened to have an opportunity to share with Amma what I was doing at OzHarvest, and he embraced the idea. He told me food was very precious, and feeding people is sacred work, and that good food is so important for people's state of mind, for their mental health. He blessed the work I was doing. It was a beautiful moment that I still treasure.

Over time, I have come to understand that a blessing is not some sort of magic spell. Amma was simply giving me a fixed moment in time that I could hold onto, forever, and remember. *Yes, Ronni, you can give yourself permission to do this. This is your sacred service. Go ahead, and go full out with it.* Over time, I came to realise that feeling blessed is simply the choice to look at what you have and be truly grateful. It is not something outside of you. It is not 'good things' happening to you. It is not something someone does to you. Being blessed is a lens. It is, quite simply, the difference between choosing to see the goodness of the man in front of you and choosing to see his faults and shortcomings. The one who chooses to see the former is blessed. The one who chooses to see the latter is not. Same person, different approach. Sometimes it just takes a person looking from the outside to remind you that your blessings are already within you. Amma was that person for me.

Many visits to Amma have followed since. With each one, I have gained a greater sense of the inner expansion that comes with service, whatever that service may be, and however it may look. And what has slowly become clearer and clearer is that no one can truly succeed alone. The joy is in getting there together. The joy is in realising that we are all made from the same stuff, that we are tied together, and that our suffering is collective, as is our joy. So when people feel something different around OzHarvest from other organisations, they are right. There is something different. There is a spirit around OzHarvest that has brought me on this journey. It is the very simple gift of doing good. Service and doing good, that is what I heard as Amma's overarching message. He opened me up to a deep sense of goodness and alignment within myself, and in so doing helped me bring something to OzHarvest that I'd never brought to any of my other ventures. There is a spirit of love and hope and energy and possibility that runs through our organisation, and no matter what you believe in or don't believe in, I think anyone involved with us can feel that, enjoys it and wants to come along for the ride.

# CHAPTER 28

# MAGIC YELLOW APRON

The pick-ups and deliveries of our first driver, in the early days of OzHarvest, were fairly sporadic. One day he'd pick up ten kilos of food, and the next he'd pick up a hundred, which would be a terribly exciting day for us. Today, OzHarvest picks up 200 tonnes of food a week. But every single bit of food we collected then was precious. And it felt so easy. We didn't have to teach anybody about our business. Everyone who heard about it wanted to donate or support because they could immediately connect with the concept of not wasting food. It made sense. The food donors just loved giving us their food. They'd never had this opportunity before. There was so much joy, and such connection with people. It was those donors who really built OzHarvest. The 'mom and pop' store owners who ran their little businesses loved the notion that they were doing something useful.

My favourite, insane thing which would often happen (and still does) was this: an agency would call and say, 'Our shelter is having a barbecue, and our funds are really low. Is there any chance you have barbecue food for us?' And I would have to say, 'I'm so sorry, but I really can't promise that we'll have barbecue food for you. We don't know what we'll get from one day to the next.' It felt awful, of course, to let them down. But then, I swear to you, the day before they needed that particular type of food, somebody would call us unexpectedly and say, 'We've had to cancel our office barbecue, can you please come and collect fifteen kilos of sausages, bread, onions and buns, including the sauce?' I cannot tell you how many times the universe has paired someone's specific food request with availability of that product. So many times. I could then call and say, 'You know how you asked for barbecue products for tomorrow? Well, we've got 'em! We'll be there!' I could cry just thinking about it. It's the best feeling. It was like we were magicians. This did of course cause a few problems, because people started calling thinking they could order food from us. And I'd have to say, 'Sorry, it doesn't work that way. We might be able to provide it, but we may not.' The miraculous fact was that more often than not, we could!

One day I decided to hold our very first OzHarvest fundraiser. I had the idea that I wanted to invite corporate businesspeople to the event by sending them an apron as a personalised invitation. I wanted them to bring that apron with them, to come and cook meals for vulnerable people. I thought an apron couldn't be a simpler symbol of service, humanity and love. But I knew that buying a hundred aprons was not in the OzHarvest budget. I sat in the office and told Elaine about my apron fantasy. And I swear to you, the words weren't even fully out of my mouth when the phone rang. It was Esther Nothman, an old friend who had a screen-printing and T-shirt business. She said, 'Ronni, I don't know if this will be of any use to you, but I've just had an order for a hundred aprons where the screen printing for the brand has gone all wrong. I was going to trash them—they are completely unusable to us—but before I do, do you want them? Honestly, I was gobsmacked. The timing was freaky. What could be more perfect than aprons? Rescued aprons! It was even better than I could have imagined. I'm risking sounding woo-woo, but honestly, I've had so many instances where it is clear to me that all you have to do sometimes is dream something up and let yourself get excited. And ask! Put it out there. Even if you're just putting it out there within yourself. Sometimes it seems there is a force in the universe that finds delight in creating a strange sense of order with our resources, if we allow it to do so.

Aprons are so significant in the life of a food charity. Here I used them as an invitation. Later on, the OzHarvest aprons became an object of magic. This is the story of the magic yellow apron. It's a story that was born from a beautiful program we run at OzHarvest, called Cooking for a Cause. It's a team-building experience that also embeds knowledge about sustainability and not wasting food. Cooking for a Cause is a sophisticated cooking class with our fabulous chefs. You make hundreds of beautiful meals from food we have rescued, then you pack it up and it is delivered to shelters, where it is used to feed people. It's a magical experience for participants.

One morning at OzHarvest, the phone rang and I heard my executive assistant, Marla, saying, 'Ronni is right here, why don't you speak to her yourself? I'll hand her over.' She handed me the phone and a woman said, 'Hi. I just really, really want to thank you for my magic yellow apron.'

'Oh?' I said. 'I knew we gave out yellow aprons at OzHarvest, but I didn't know they were *magic* yellow aprons. Can you tell me why it's a magic yellow apron?'

She said, 'I came to Cooking for a Cause with a bunch of people recently. I don't really socialise. I live on my own, and have been very lonely for a while. But I came to Cooking for a Cause, and we were given this yellow apron, and through the class we learnt new skills and I had the best time. The next day, I put on my yellow apron at home, and on day one, I was Neil Perry. And I cooked a meal and then I knocked on my neighbour's door and gave it to them. They loved it! And then the next day I was Kylie Kwong. I cooked and called some people over, and it was really special to share a meal with them. And then the next day I was Matt Moran. I've been every single celebrity chef of my choosing. And my life has changed because I'm sharing food, and people are coming into my life, and it's all because of my magic yellow apron.'

'Well,' I replied, 'that's the most beautiful thing I have ever heard. And from now on, nobody will be given a yellow apron. Everybody will be given a magic yellow apron, because then they'll be able to do whatever they like with that apron. It will create their magic.' The magic yellow apron. What a way to change lives!

This woman changed my life a little with her newfound magic. Her story summed up so much of what my vision for OzHarvest is about. It also embodies my own life vision. It's about sharing, and it's about reaching out to one another, even when the divides between us seem insurmountable. It's about being brave and bold and having fun. And it's about knowing that today you can choose to do and be whatever or whomever you want, in big and small ways, but in ways that are significant. And it's about food! Food as a facilitator of togetherness. Food as a peace giver. Food as the tapestry of our lives. I'm so grateful that by recognising her magic, she helped me see my own. And she helped each person who ate her food feel and see their own magic too. Imagination has its own limitless power, and one magic yellow apron goes a long way when you discover the enriching power of giving.

The power of giving is always more present at Christmas time. We have bountiful food donations. People are winding down and closing their businesses, and there are so many parties that the quality and quantity of leftover food is amazing. But the time between Christmas Day and New Year's Day is always challenging. During this time, scarcity and aloneness are felt by many in our society. You can go through a whole year surviving, but the minute the holidays hit, people in vulnerable situations feel it a whole lot more. Advertising everywhere promotes joy and abundance, and it becomes a painful time for many people.

OzHarvest delivers directly to many charitable organisations that service vulnerable people. They, in turn, give our food to those people. But just when you'd think people need charitable organisations the most, those shelters close during Christmas, or work with a skeleton staff, which is understandable. Often, however, the people who live in these shelters have to move out at this time. Many homeless people ride on a train for the entire holiday season, because it's a safe, warm place to live and escape. They go up and down the same train lines. It takes them out of the city and away from a painful place. When the train closes, they might sleep at a station until the next train. So not only are they hungry and lonely, but all their normal support systems and services completely break down.

It's also particularly around Christmas time that people who have found themselves in difficult circumstances reach out. People can fall through the cracks in a moment, people who have never imagined it could happen to them. With the change of a few circumstances—a partner leaving, a death in a family, the loss of a job, a traumatic incident, bankruptcy, illness—that person could be you or me. It may come as a surprise to some, but even in an abundant country like Australia, people are falling through the cracks all the time. I want to share a couple of letters that left a powerful impression on me.

*Hi there,*

*Could you tell me how my family could be helped with food? My kids and I have only $25 left after rent and bills for food, nappies, medical/education expenses, etc. This week we've been helped by some friends and a charitable organisation with food, but in a couple of weeks we will be back to eating rice, soup and bread. It's not an ideal diet for three growing children.*

*I wonder if my children could possibly be treated to a meal that they deserve rather than what they normally get? They are good kids who rarely complain. I'm applying for jobs constantly but not even an interview yet. It is very disheartening.*

*I feel like I am failing my children. We went from a happy family living on a FIFO (fly-in, fly-out) income to one that is struggling* due to my husband leaving us for someone else. I can't ask for more wonderful kids—they are my delight! Sorry for the sob story, I don't want sympathy. All I want is something better for my kids—a treat to show how much they are worth and that they are not forgotten. Thank you for reading.

Hello and Merry Christmas,

I am emailing you with my fingers crossed as a last-minute chance that someone out there may be able to help myself and my little family, as I have failed them.

It's Monday afternoon and Christmas is four days away. We have absolutely nothing. No presents, no food and no hope. We're a family of four—two adults and two children. We don't have a Christmas tree. We can't even afford gas and electricity. To be honest, I don't know if we'll have running electricity on Christmas. I've hit rock bottom.

We survive on two government benefits to get by. We have been working to get my significant other carer's benefits and also disability benefits for myself. I suffer from severe depression, anxiety and PTSD, to name a few issues. At the moment, our benefits just cover our rent, fuel and a few groceries, if we're lucky.

We have our gas bill owing, our electricity bill owing and we can't drive our car as we have not been able to afford to get it reregistered. We don't even have mobile phone credit. Our only contact to the outside world right now is via our home internet, which is also due.

Can someone please help us? I'm scared, and I can only imagine what my partner is feeling. It's tough but I'm extremely emotional.

*What can I do? Is this the end? Do I literally give up? I love my family with all of my heart and I have failed them.*

*Please, please, please. If you can—PLEASE HELP ME SOMEHOW.*

After reading these letters, I knew I needed our donors to understand who was receiving their food. I'd felt for a long time that, in particular, supermarket managers and staff had no connection whatsoever to what was happening with their surplus food once we took it from their loading dock. This was obvious from the way they treated their surplus. Sometimes they kept it for us very carefully, sometimes they didn't, and we'd see it in their loading dock bins. It was so random and I felt that if they knew what was going on behind the scenes, it might make a huge difference. I called our supermarket donors and said, 'I'd like to come in and talk to your managers. I have something to share with them.' They said, 'Of course.'

Within a few days I was standing in front of twenty store managers and reading these letters to them. They were in tears. I think it was the first time that they had put two and two together— that their food made all the difference in the world, to so many people. The behaviour in those stores changed after that day. The amount of food was consistent, there was lots of it, it was beautiful quality and it was easy to collect. Hearing from the mouths of people who were receiving their food had enabled these managers to find a profound head and heart connection. Working from your head alone simply accomplishes the basics. When the heart comes in, many things change. Our hearts are our momentum for action. You become willing, you become aligned, you become capable; you are driven and inspired. It's a wonderful thing to witness.

And, by the way, in both cases of the above letters, as well as many others, OzHarvest jumped into action. I had the lucky job of delivering presents, Christmas trees, food, hampers, ongoing supplies and hugs! We connected them to other organisations and ensured that they were looked after. These were Christmas miracles in action.

One night, I was walking around at the Sydney night noodle market. We were doing a fundraiser for OzHarvest where we'd offer a fortune cookie in exchange for a donation. I was approaching people with my donation bucket and cookies, when a guy came up to me, put a few bucks in and said, 'You don't know me, but I've never been so proud to put money into something. When I was down and out, I got food from you. And no, I won't take a fortune cookie. I want to keep it for someone else. But I want you to know I've turned my life around. Thank you.'

And with that he walked off. Big little miracles are around us all the time.

# CHAPTER 29

# BYZANTINE BUREAUCRACY

OzHarvest had been running for a year now and we were plenty busy. I was being interviewed on radio a lot at this point, and it was creating awareness, which was powerful. I'd get all sorts of interesting calls and good things were happening. A wonderful lawyer, Bruce Cutler, heard me on the radio and decided to volunteer for OzHarvest one day a week. He was also very well connected in the Law Council, and I didn't know then how beneficial that would be. People's generosity is a beautiful, astounding thing.

One day, someone called us and said, 'We'd love to give you food, but we can't because we're not allowed to.'

'What do you mean?' I asked. They then explained that from a legal perspective, they were liable for any food they gave us. If someone became ill after eating their food, they would be in trouble. Well, we had enough food being donated to keep us very busy. But I realised this law meant that we wouldn't be able to tap into bigger sources of food in the future. I kept learning that there was more food being thrown away, and I did not want any obstacles in the way of people being able to give, or for us to be able to receive it. I certainly didn't want someone to put their food in the bin for fear of being liable for it. I knew then and there we had to fix this. It was quite bizarre that I'd got this far and it was the first time anyone had brought this to my attention.

I called Harland again, my high-powered lawyer. We met in his boardroom, with his five lawyers, and we talked about the status of the laws pertaining to safe food handling, liability and the Good Samaritan Act—which is the law that exempts legal liability from an act that has been done in good faith. I discovered that the civil liabilities law at the time stated that you could give away food to anyone, but you would be liable if they got ill. In other words, if a pizza place gave us a pizza, and we gave it to someone and they got sick, the pizza place was liable. The responsibility (or the onus) was on them, not on us. This was not going to work for us if we wanted to rescue *all* food, and it certainly made the act of giving a potential risk for our donors. It was because of this law that no other charity was touching fresh produce—they were only prepared to deal with dry goods.

Apparently, someone had tried to change this law before, but it had become too hard, and the case had been dropped. Harland and one of his team members, Liz Grey, worked tirelessly, pro bono. They began pulling together laws, and started lobbying on behalf of OzHarvest. Lobbying is not easy. It's completely and utterly doable, but it's not easy. It takes perseverance and it takes having the right people on board—that's the bottom line. It also takes finding a champion in government who is willing to fight that fight with you, and stand up for it, and help push the motion through. Liz, in particular, had exceptional people skills and was a huge asset in the day-to-day liaison with government.

I'd be badgering Harland many times a week: 'Is there any progress?' I'd say.

He'd update me: 'Ronni, we're hitting some curly bits. We're dealing with a Byzantine bureaucracy. We're trying to do something a bit radical! OzHarvest is motivated by the heart, but government bureaucrats aren't. It's really about managing these "opposites". Have patience. This will take time.'

It was a nail-biting race to the finish line. Some days it felt really possible, and other days we thought it would never happen. But our team kept working; they persevered and persevered. What we had on our side was the evidence that OzHarvest had been running for a whole year, and that people really wanted to give us their food. We gave it our total push and waited with bated breath.

Exactly one year later, in late 2005, the Civil Liabilities Act of New South Wales was amended, enabling food donors to give their food away in good faith for a charitable or benevolent purpose, without fear of liability. The recipient must receive that food for free and the food must be safe to consume and follow safe food handling and hygiene standards. Then, in 2008, my volunteer Bruce Cutler saved the day, as he and his friends on the Law Council took on other states on our behalf. By late 2009, we had succeeded in the Australian Capital Territory, Queensland and South Australia. Thankfully, Victoria already had a Good Samaritan law. Based on the precedent set in New South Wales, it became the norm in other states, which was gratifying.

My team was so competent, so incredible, and I was blown away. It was such a big deal for us. We could now accept food from everywhere and everyone. It fundamentally changed the rule book by which anyone could give away food. This meant that when we were approached by Virgin Airlines in 2014, in relation to their surplus food, we could take it. Sandwiches, fruit and vegetables, cheese and crackers—the lot, and Qantas followed suit. We're still working on collecting their yoghurt! No other country in the world has been allowed to rescue food from a domestic airline yet. The civil liabilities amendment made this situation possible. It changed the nature of food rescue for the whole country, and I am truly proud of Australia for recognising the need for change and granting us this victory.

CHAPTER 30

# FISHTAILS AND POTATO SKINS

In 2005, OzHarvest prepared to host a dinner fundraiser, where we invited a hundred business leaders to share a meal of rescued food. I asked five well-known Australian chefs to jump on board, mates from my catering world, to create a beautiful gourmet three-course dinner, sourced from surplus food. In the lead-up to the night, we had asked the chefs to take part in a nose-to-tail practice, in preparation for the banquet. This meant keeping every useful scrap from their restaurant cooking, to use for the event. On the night, they would utilise the off cuts from fish and meat, bones, vegetable stalks and so on.

The dinner came around and everything was looking gorgeous, and just before the meal was served I stood up to tell the guests how excited we were to host this event, and to share this beautiful, quality food with them, prepared by these amazing chefs. I explained it was surplus food, and everything was sustainably sourced. Then I finished my spiel with, 'Any questions?'

The first hand went up and someone said, 'I'm very nervous about eating leftovers. Aren't we going to get sick?'

The next hand went up. 'What does surplus actually mean?'

The third hand was raised. 'Why would we want to eat rescued food?'

Lots more hands started going up with similar concerns. It turns out a lot of people were feeling uncomfortable.

What an interesting insight I had at that moment. People didn't necessarily know what we were talking about. There had been a big gap in the food-rescue discourse. I had to explain that the food was not leftovers from someone's plate, it was untouched produce that food outlets had been unable to use. If I hadn't sufficiently succeeded in calming every single person down after that, the proof was in the rescued bread-and-butter pudding, because it turned out to be an absolute gourmet feast. The chefs had created inspired dishes from their leftover food, from incredible ceviche, to fried fish tails with herb-stalk dressing, vegetable-stalk tempura, potato skins with dips, carrot-peel cake—the works.

Let me be clear about what surplus food means. Surplus food is anything from bread, milk, butter and cheese to fish, meat, fruit, vegetables, pasta, flour, oil, salt, spices—anything that's unopened, has been safely handled and is within the use-by date. There are many places where food waste is generated, such as corporate events, hotels, stadiums, farms, supermarkets, airlines and factories, to name just a few. Let me give you some real-life examples:

The weather was bad at a coffee festival on the weekend where they thought they'd sell 100,000 cups of coffee, but instead they sold 50,000 cups. They now have 5000 litres of leftover milk. They call us.

The letter 'C' is printed incorrectly on 10,000 cereal packets. They call us.

A supermarket changes the packaging on their pasta line. They need to stock their shelf with the newly labelled products. They have pallets and pallets of the previously labelled pasta left over. They call us.

The Sydney Convention Centre is having an event where they are expecting 5000 people and only 3000 show up. They have 2000 freshly made sandwiches left over. They call us.

A cricket tournament draws, wrapping up after three days instead of five. A couple of days' worth of food, for thousands of people, is left over. They call us.

Mistakenly, two people in the same supermarket put through the same order of 30,000 eggs. Suddenly they have 60,000 eggs. They call us.

An ice-cream manufacturer's freezer breaks down at their headquarters. They have tonnes and tonnes of ice-cream to rescue. They call us—that one made a hell of a lot of people happy!

It's the end of *MasterChef*, or *My Kitchen Rules* or *The Chefs' Line*, and they are closing for the season but they have a pantry stocked to the hilt with the best of everything, from macadamia oil to truffle salt. They are closing the studio kitchen for three months between seasons, and instead of trashing the surplus food, they call us.

All of the above examples cost businesses, and our economy, billions of dollars. And that's even before we take into account hiring a person to drive to the site, burn through petrol and dump the leftover kilos in landfill—which is where this food would have ended up if we hadn't rescued it. But the biggest cost of all, which means a lot more to us than money, is what it is costing the planet. Food waste is literally costing us the earth.

What I didn't know when I started OzHarvest—but it didn't take me long to find out—is that not only was OzHarvest tackling the social issue of feeding hungry people, it was also preventing good food from going to landfill. When food is trapped in landfill and starts rotting, it emits methane, a powerful greenhouse gas that is a major contributor to climate change. The best option is not to waste food in the first place. But if you happen to find a lettuce in the back of your fridge that has turned to sludge, avoid sending it to landfill. You could do that through a home compost bin, a worm farm or by taking your food waste to community gardens with a composting scheme.

Food waste in the home is quite a simple issue to overcome if you put your mind and heart to it. At OzHarvest, we developed a mantra: Look. Buy. Store. Cook. These four simple habits can help you reduce your household food waste. *Look* at what you have before you go shopping. *Buy* only what you need. *Store* food correctly. And, *cook* with what you have. And most definitely eat your leftovers! Believe it or not, this will save you money. Research from the New South Wales Environmental Program shows that the average household wastes about $3800 worth of food per year. It's easy to think that climate change is an issue that requires only government intervention. But the part we each play in our home in reducing our food waste really does count. Each of us plays a fundamental role in restoring our planet.

If food waste was a country, it would be the third biggest emitter of methane gas after the United States and China. Zero food waste is the goal, to protect our environment and distribute resources. It is gratifying to work with supermarkets, manufacturers and food producers who are committed to this goal. For example, when a supermarket has meat dated 'best before' the tenth of the month, and it hasn't sold by the eighth, they can freeze it to extend its life for us. We can then deliver it frozen, and our recipients can choose when they use it. It's a small start, but a start nonetheless to dealing with excess food, and it's a smart way for them to do business while doing good for our society.

I believe that unless businesses adopt sustainable practices and showcase their values and greater purpose—whatever that business may be, whatever that greater purpose may be—they will not last in the long run. It's what people want. The time for being in business simply to make money for stakeholders is coming to a close. We, the citizens, are beginning to demand more. We are ready.

# CHAPTER 31

# JEWEL IN THE CROWN

The question I am asked most often in interviews is: 'What is the biggest challenge you've faced in the journey of setting up OzHarvest?' For years I always gave the same answer: changing the liability laws. But in truth, if I'm to dig a little deeper, my biggest lessons initially came from having to navigate the unexpected framework of functioning within a board. Nothing could have been a steeper learning curve. It gave me the building blocks to own who I am and to learn how to lead from a place of humility.

At the inception of OzHarvest, while I was still officially under Julie's prickly, fabulous wing, she told me I needed to find a board. She told me that a board is a legal body established to ensure correct governance of any public entity, and OzHarvest was now becoming a public entity. I wasn't sure what a board entailed, as I had run RKED as a sole trader for the past fifteen years, but I thought I had a rough gist of what was required. *This won't be hard*, I thought, *I roughly need three to five people who will say yes*. So I just started asking. I had no understanding of how fundamentally important these people would be for my charity. I asked almost everyone I came into contact with—uncles, aunts, friends, my neighbour, my hairdresser, my dog, a pastor I was donating food to. You name them, I asked them.

Well, that was embarrassing, because the minute I brought my brilliant and experienced brother-in-law, Anthony, on to the board as our first ever chairman, he said, 'WHAT HAVE YOU DONE? These people don't make sense. A board is a legal body! Public funds will go into OzHarvest and the board needs to be able to protect the framework and purpose for which this organisation has been set up, as well as connect you to other valuable and influential people. Do you really know this pastor?'

Of course, I didn't! I didn't know him from a bar of soap. I barely knew what *I* was doing, let alone what *he* did. With my tail between my legs, I sheepishly had to un-invite everyone from my blundering board before we'd even started. (I didn't even have the pastor's phone number, so I had to hunt him down personally!) And then I had to look for a board all over again. This time, I chose people based on their skill set, as per Anthony's guidance—a legal person, a well-connected person, a marketing person, an accountant, and so on. Together, we brought on the 'right' people—three men and three women, including me. We were ready to go.

Within a few months, OzHarvest began to be a very attractive story to the media. There were a few things that ignited the interest of the press, and people in general. Firstly, they were very interested in the businesswoman-turns-social-entrepreneur part. I had gone from owning my own business to creating this passion project. And I was not young. That was novel too. But it was the cause itself that ignited them most of all. The notion of rescuing surplus food to feed hungry people made so much sense. I now call it my 'universal truth'. People don't require any convincing. It was an OMG moment, *Why has nobody ever done this in Australia?* And it only added to the story that it took a passionate woman who'd been running a business, who required a solution to this problem, to implement this idea here.

The board was highly involved in the day-to-day running of the business. As I was still running RKED full-time, I was very reliant on their support. They were following due process and I could see they were aiming at slowly and steadily building a respectable food-rescue charity. But I felt I was not a good public representative of this slow and steady pace.

I brought an energetic quality to OzHarvest that seemed attractive to the public and press. I was talking openly and emotionally about purpose and meaning and, fifteen years ago, people were not talking about connecting head and heart in a business context. I don't think this was what the board had in mind for the face of OzHarvest.

I also had zero experience with board meetings. I had no idea what it meant to be accountable in the context of a boardroom. I didn't come prepared with copious notes of what had happened the month before, and I didn't have board reports. I was flying by the seat of my pants. And I can understand this created a huge level of frustration for them. They recognised my strengths, and they totally believed in the idea of OzHarvest. But when it came down to it, my personality didn't quite fit the bill. I was not trained in a business framework, I was not conservative enough and I was too emotional. I think it was exasperating for them and it was challenging for me.

Some days I'd just crumple in those board meetings. I'd be easily moved to tears if I felt they didn't value me, and that felt so uncomfortable in the context of a business roundtable. Allowing myself that level of emotion—though I don't feel I can help it—has confounded men and women alike who have been associated with OzHarvest. Would I have felt differently about how my emotions may have been perceived if I had been male? I don't think these qualities worked in my favour on the board, yet I didn't think to make myself appear tougher to achieve what I needed to do or where I needed to go. I never even considered playing that game. I brought myself as I was. Now I see that has been one of my strengths. At the time, however, it felt like a weakness.

For the first six years, navigating the board was my biggest challenge. I was too sensitive and continually felt I could not fulfil their conservative image of the founder of a charity. But I was exhilarated by the cause and that kept me going, despite these feelings. It would have been easier to give up and walk away. To say, 'I've done what I could, and now it's too hard.' Many people have walked into my office since and shared a similar story with me. Trust me, I understand. I did not feel right, look right, act right, or contain myself enough for a whole bunch of people who mattered to me. I would have changed if I'd known how. I knew there was a box I was supposed to fit into, I just didn't exactly know what the box looked like and how I could fit myself into it. My way was working for the growth of OzHarvest, but it also caused a lot of tension.

I could have allowed it to defeat me, but I believe that when you are acting from a place of calling, strength comes. That does not mean it didn't hurt, or that I didn't take things personally. But, somehow, I had the *sitzfleisch* (the Yiddish word for 'sitting flesh'). It meant I had to sit with my uncomfortable feelings a lot, and learn what I needed to without becoming defensive.

At this point, I was still working at RKED full time, and had been doing OzHarvest voluntarily for almost seven years. People can't quite believe that I was fronting something so public and had another job as well. It became challenging to juggle both. Naturally, RKED received less and less work because I was less interested in the hustle, and more on a mission to rescue every bit of food I could find. Yet I had never intended to be paid to run OzHarvest, and due to that, I hadn't considered closing down RKED. I was keeping my event business afloat because I needed it financially. I couldn't do one business without the other.

Then, in 2009, something happened that changed the game for me. I was invited to apply for the Vodafone World of Difference program, which unfortunately no longer exists. It was created to support socially conscientious people to answer their true calling by offering them the opportunity to work in a charity of their choice for a year— on the condition that they give up their full-time work. It came with a year's salary of $50,000. The program also provided mentoring and guided leadership.

To my complete shock, I was one of four people who won! I was probably the oldest winner of that prize—I was in my fifties—but

I didn't even remember to feel old. What did that matter? I was just doing what I needed and wanted to be doing. To this day, I'm extremely grateful. It was a momentous experience to win that prize, and a huge decision to accept it. I knew it would mean closing the doors to RKED permanently. It couldn't run without me for a year, and I couldn't expect to close a business for a year and then rebuild it a year later. It was madly insecure and risky, with no certainty or security that I would have a job either at OzHarvest or any other business after the end of that year. And yet, I knew this was a little parachute. This prize would allow me to take the leap, the plunge, into running OzHarvest full time. It was now or never. I would have to take it day by day, and worry about financial security later.

It wasn't easy ending my time at RKED. Colin and I cried. We had shared so much together, had spent so many years side by side. It was a family business, with many wonderful clients. It had provided for me and my family for many years. I couldn't sell it, because the business was built around my name. I simply gave away my props and the furniture to a charity, and closed the beautiful warehouse door that had marked so many unique moments in the lives of so many people. Colin and I parted ways as business colleagues for good.

My Vodafone year of difference certainly paid off. During that year, OzHarvest catapulted into the mainstream, as our programs were highlighted through the myriad of press that came with the Vodafone award. We launched new programs. We now had ten vans on the road. We celebrated delivering five million meals. We expanded our reach to Canberra and Newcastle. At the end of that year, to my complete surprise, I was chosen as one of four Australians of the Year by the Australian government. It was an incredible, unexpected honour to receive this prize from the Prime Minister of Australia. Exciting things were happening.

As I finished my Vodafone journey, a new board began its term at OzHarvest. I thought I'd need to find a new job, but before I had a chance to consider my options, the new board asked me to stay on. They had witnessed what had happened for OzHarvest during my year of taking on the role full time. It was decided that I would move on from being the unofficial face and leader of the organisation, to officially taking on the paid role of CEO and founder. I never went back to event coordination as a business. From that day on I brought events to OzHarvest. In terms of ability, capacity and joy, being full time at OzHarvest was beyond my wildest dreams.

I have learnt so much about growing a business since those early days, from working with a board to building relationships with staff, volunteers and stakeholders. I have learnt that boards do not have to like or agree with everything you do. Respectful disagreement does not negate mutual respect and harmony. If they don't agree, there may be a good reason for it, and that is exactly the kind of difference in judgement that you need to rely on, because at all times you are acting on their behalf and they on yours, each having the best interests of the organisation at heart. Differences in opinion do not mean that you are incapable or have done something wrong. What a relief to have finally understood that and to realise that the board forms a broad coterie of wisdom to tap into at every opportunity. Residing in that place of complicit generosity works for everyone.

Ah, beginnings, middles and endings. They don't necessarily look anything like one another. If you are at the beginning of a venture, just know that this beginning isn't necessarily how the middle is going to look, or how the end will unfold. I hope this is a comfort, if you are finding your beginning rough. I bumbled along for quite a while, making many mistakes. Despite not seeming like the perfect candidate to build OzHarvest on paper, in fact I was and still am. What is obvious to me now is that there is no perfect candidate. There is only you, and if you want to do something, you are the perfect candidate. All you really need is the courage to start and the rest will unfold.

It was only many years later that, very suddenly, I remembered something Helen from Angel Harvest had said to me. This memory took me back to our meeting, sipping tea in my sister's living room. After she had asked me about my agenda, she said, 'I want you to know that the board is the jewel in your crown. They represent the organisation; take nothing personally.' I heard her. But at the time, I didn't understand what she meant.

# CHAPTER 32

# TAKE WHAT YOU NEED, GIVE IF YOU CAN

Maybe it's the undying socialist in me, birthed during those early kibbutz days, but I've always wondered about the best way to take care of the greater community, to create a place where needs are met, simply and easily. The way OzHarvest runs is to take food to charities and for the charities to give that food directly to those who need it most. Yet to be a recipient of a charity means registering. There's a whole system, a whole process that's required in order to sign up. I loved visiting the charities and seeing the food distributed, but I had always thought to myself, *What must it feel like to have to register and go through all that red tape?* Many people would find that process confronting. They may have a roof over their head, but may not have enough money after all their expenses for food. Some people may feel embarrassed to seek out support. For a long time, I wondered how OzHarvest could share food differently, to reach those whose needs were not being met through charities, to create a place where resources are shared with no strings attached.

Then one day I had the idea of a free supermarket. What a beautiful way to take care of people who need food and can't afford it. Of course, a few weeks after this, in 2016, I was in France and I stumbled upon a free mini supermarket. I was so excited; I couldn't believe it! But it didn't take long till I realised it was exactly everything I *didn't* want for my dream supermarket. This was a free supermarket—yes—but people had to show their stamp, show their 'neediness' credentials, and then they could only take three items, there was a discounted price for other items. It had all these rules. And when I saw all that, my heart sank. I thought, *I want to have a supermarket that anybody can come to. I want a place where no one has to register, where you can just take what you need, and you can be treated with the utmost dignity and respect.*

Shortly after that, a motel became available in the Sydney suburb of Kensington, and the owner—TOGA Group, a long-time supporter of OzHarvest—came to us and asked us what could be done with it on a temporary basis. TOGA Group is a family-owned property development company whose owners have a passion for social justice and wanted to make a contribution and work with vulnerable youth. Now the foyer of this motel had been a restaurant. So they said, 'If we house vulnerable people in the building, would you fix up the restaurant and turn it into a place to feed the people in the building?' I went to look at the restaurant and it was appalling. It was filthy. It was abandoned and gross.

I said, 'No, this is completely unusable as a restaurant, unless you're willing to gut it and redo it. But if you just gut it, could we open a free supermarket so those people in the building can use it?

Ultimately, it could be a supermarket that's open to anybody.' Well, they loved the idea. They said they would clear it out and paint it for us. It was happening.

When I told my staff at OzHarvest what we were going to do, they said, 'Hang on, what do you mean?'

'It's a free supermarket,' I said. 'All the produce is free and we need to fill it up, fill the shelves, make it work. Let's do it!' They stared at me. There was panic in their eyes. I mean, they did love the idea, but I could tell they were nervous about implementing it. It's true, I had never run a supermarket. I didn't really say how we'd run it on a daily basis, because I had no idea how we would run it yet. But I wasn't worried. They are amazing people, and I knew they would figure it out. And so would I!

Firstly, I called Harris Farm, a local supermarket chain, and they immediately said, 'We have leftover shelving that you could repurpose.' The space suddenly felt like a supermarket. Then we called Joe Thorp who used to work for Hoshizaki, a commercial refrigeration business that had kindly donated to us many, many times before, and he arranged to provide fridges for the super-market. And then, of course, we realised that what we desperately needed was a supermarket manager. I decided to call our partners at Woolworths, but I felt the people I spoke to put it in the too-hard basket. I knew that if I spoke to Brad Banducci, the CEO, everything would change. He would love it.

I finally got onto him. I said, 'Brad, we're opening a free super-market. I've suggested the idea to your staff but it's taking too long. Would it be possible to second me a supermarket manager?' He said, 'Ronni, of course. I love this idea.' And from that point on,

Woolworths ran with the idea and brought in the ideal candidate, Megan Jordan, taking her out of her managerial role at one of their branches and sending her to us, at their expense. Whoever was instrumental in choosing Megan had tremendous insight, because we could not have found a more perfect person to run the OzHarvest Market. Megan had experienced homelessness as a young girl. She'd turned her life around, and she brought an extraordinary level of compassion to our venture. She was so smart, she knew when to be firm and when to be gentle with the clientele, and I couldn't have asked for a more incredible person.

In the meantime, we were trying to make sure all the wording for the concept of the supermarket was right. The words were very important to me. First, we came up with the phrase, 'Take what you need; give what you can'. But something didn't feel right to me. And then I realised it implied you had to give to take. I didn't like that. I decided it should be, 'Take what you need; give *if* you can', because it should be your choice. If you can, you can. And if you can't, you can't. The whole premise and philosophy was that anybody could walk through the door. Anybody could take. If you have money, put it in the box. There would be no till and there would be no cash register. There would be no scales and there would be no waste. There would be no bags either, simply what you could fit in your own bags, or in your own hands. This would mean anybody could have access to food—without any explanations, without having to justify a single thing. It would be about dignity and respect. It would be a place for anybody and everybody. This place would be an equaliser.

The OzHarvest Market inauguration day came around and I arrived at this beautiful yellow-and-black space. The shelves were completely stocked with fresh food, toothbrushes, toiletries, cosmetics, canned food, dry goods, nappies, flowers, cookies, nuts, bread, meat—you name it. We had collected everything that is in a supermarket from the surplus of our supermarket donors. The place had been beautifully designed and branded for us by Frost Design. The front door had a heart painted on it. I had known they were doing that, but what I hadn't realised was that because it was a sliding door, every time you went in, the heart opened. You walked straight into the chamber of an open heart. It was genius! I stood there in awe, I walked in. I cried, of course. It was phenomenal. The vision had come to life more spectacularly than I could have imagined.

On our first day, there was a queue around the block. People from all walks of life came to visit. People who needed food; people who wanted to check it out, who were curious; people who were locals; and people who had travelled a long distance. We had and still have 350 people a day who come to do their free shopping. They come from far and wide. In the first year, a lot of people came just to check out the place and put money in our donation box. People walked right in, checked it out, and threw $10, $20, $50 in the box as an acknowledgement of our work. We were gobsmacked. In that first year, we raised $60,000, just from the money in our little yellow box. We could not believe the generosity.

Nobody, in a million years, could have imagined the kind of publicity that would come from doing this. The people at TOGA Group were completely blown away. No marketing budget they'd ever spent had brought them such goodness. It received so much attention, as it's such an important place; there is nowhere else in Australia that you can literally walk in and not have to prove anything, and be treated with such care. Every other 'free' supermarket has membership fees, cost structures, registrations, 'specials' on certain foods. But this was completely different. Every journalist wanted to talk to us about it, hundreds of them. And every time they contacted us, without fail, they asked, 'How on earth will this work? People will take advantage of this; they will take more than they need!' This had never even occurred to me. But I thought, *You know what? If people do take advantage, maybe that is why they are here. They clearly need it. They may have a problem in their life and they may need support. And if they can afford things and come here because they don't want to pay for it, then they clearly have a problem too. I can't ban people simply because they have a problem. This is a place that welcomes everyone. Nobody has to register, nobody has to tell us why they are there. Anybody can come through. Anybody can take. And anybody can give.* I thought, *Let's just see what happens!*

What we did find was that a tiny handful of people weren't as thoughtful as others. So we started a personalised shopping experience, to manage the inventory and make everyone feel special. The veggies are the items that go most quickly. Then the fruit and the meat. We often don't have much of that. They are the things we have to be mindful about sharing out the most. We approach each person and ask how many people they feed in their family. If someone wanted to take seven packets of pasta and there were two people in their family, we'd say, 'Please take two packets and come back another time if you need more. We want to have enough left on the shelves for other people today.' It's all about sharing. The purpose of the supermarket is to share produce and to be mindful. We find people leave fully satisfied this way. And at the end of the day there is nothing left on the shelves. They're empty. There is no waste. It turns out our little free supermarket was and is a roaring success. We've had people from over 50 countries reach out to us to replicate the model back home. The TOGA Group had given us the space for a year, and at the time of writing this we are now in our third year.

We also noticed that many hungry people were coming in. They were eating the produce before it reached their baskets. In fact, they were absolutely starving. So we created a side room where nutritious food is available every day. The volunteers who work in the market make sandwiches, cakes, cut fresh fruit and vegetables— all rescued and made with love. We make soup in winter. If people are hungry, they are welcome to come and sit and chill before or after their shop. It's an inviting community space.

We now have a specific van and driver just for the supermarket. And the supermarket requires more food than our biggest charity drop-off. The shelves have to be full at the beginning of each day. Our produce comes from everywhere. From Woolworths, from other supermarkets, from whoever calls us with excess food. The Bread & Butter project is one of our most inspiring providers. This business trains refugees to bake, giving people an incredible opportunity to make a living, baking the sublime bread that they sell. When they heard about the supermarket, they rang us straight away and said, we have surplus bread each day! And so, every single day of the week we have delicious bread from them.

Possibly the other most extraordinary aspect of our supermarket is that, aside from the supermarket manager, the whole place is staffed by volunteers. To fill a roster of ten people a day, five days a week, is no small feat. The supermarket is only open from

10.00 a.m. to 2.00 p.m. Tuesday to Friday, but we need ten volunteers a day, and we need them for five days to clean and fill the shelves. There is much work to be done running a supermarket! Some volunteers have been there from the beginning, some come and go, some are new. But the volunteers just continue to show up, day in, day out. I am in absolute awe of them. And if someone doesn't show up, a call out goes out and one of us from the office goes to work at the supermarket. It doesn't happen very often. But it happens. And when it does, it's a total treat.

If you want to hear some of the remarkable stories that unfold in our supermarket, speak to one of our volunteers. There are thousands of stories. I have witnessed quite a few myself, but this one is my favourite.

I was at the supermarket one day and a woman in a hijab came in with her two beautiful children. She saw me and came straight to me and said, 'Oh, I just need you to know that my husband just lost his job, otherwise I would never have to do this.'

I said, 'Stop. I'm really, really sorry that your husband lost his job. But in this space, you don't have to tell me anything. I don't need to know that. Anybody can come here. Now let's go shopping!'

It was after Easter, and we had boxes of gorgeous cookies and other special sweets. And when we reached a huge stack of cookies, the little boy pulled on his mother's dress and said, 'Mummy I think this shop is too expensive for us.' At which point I said, 'This is a different kind of shop. Now let's put lots of these in your basket!'

And then we continued walking through, and when we got to the end, after she'd put everything from our basket into her own bags, she stopped at the counter. There was no cash register, no anything, just a yellow box that said, 'Every dollar donated to OzHarvest allows two meals to be delivered.' She opened her wallet, took out five dollars, and said, 'Boys, we've just allowed ten meals to be donated.' By this stage I was bawling, everyone around me was bawling, we all hugged, she turned around and was gone.

My heart is filled to the brim when I think about the precious nature of the lesson this wise mother taught her kids. Because even though this was a charity for them, she realised the most powerful piece of the puzzle was that they were still able to contribute by the act of giving back to someone else. On that day, this woman and her children created a better world. They were participants in a greater care economy, part of the perfect cycle of giving and receiving that is not always easy for us to understand. The act of receiving became an act of empowerment. She understood that every single one of us has that power. To me, there is no greater or more powerful embodiment of an act of charity than this.

# CHAPTER 33

# BOTTLING THE BRAND

People often ask me how OzHarvest built such a strong brand. They are baffled by how rescuing food became so sexy. How did our organisation evolve from rescuing surplus food to collaborating with some of the world's greatest chefs? How did we attract global businesses to support us? The answer is multilayered, but I believe it was a convergence of elements and timing that came together exquisitely, much like an improvised rescue recipe, where quality ingredients are thrown together in an innovative way to create a delicious dish.

To create a commercial brand, you would need to spend millions of dollars and hope you hit the right tone and that people respond: 'Buy this perfume and you will feel alluring.' In our case, we chose to share our compelling cause and truthfully discuss the story behind our impact and the lives we'd touched. This created a unifying proposition and a narrative that attracted stakeholders, as well as values that inspired the right people to join our team. 'Come and work with us, and you will make other people feel amazing, and you will end up feeling amazing too.'

It's interesting that from our first day—and I'm not quite sure how—we seemed to always punch above our weight. We only had one van in our first year, yet people would say to me, 'I see your vans absolutely everywhere!' But it was only one van, spinning around like a top, darting all over the place! We were highly visible, and this was even before we could afford to turn that first white van into a bright yellow beacon. We were completely nondescript, except that our van had our cause emblazoned on it: 'Rescuing Food to Feed Those in Need'. People would call me and ask, 'Is that what you *really* do? What does it mean? How can I support you?' The cause was captivating right from the get-go. It was only later, when we turned our fleet yellow, that we became a bit like bees buzzing around the place. That's basically what every company wants: for people to recognise you from a distance and smile when they see you coming! I think that is so important, to spread sunshine around the place.

It felt the same when I was doing my first interviews. I think many journalists thought I was talking to them from the OzHarvest headquarters, but it was just me in my RKED office, juggling press amidst the next wedding I was organising. Food rescue captured everyone's imagination. The transparency of our cause—that one single dollar delivered two meals to someone in need—was incredibly powerful. Nobody else was showing that one single dollar could stretch so far. People were thrilled with the notion that someone had finally done this. I had so many people telling me they had thought to do it before me, but they had never got around to it. It seemed I was tapping into a problem that people knew about and felt deeply about, but had done nothing about. It was time. People wanted this. People were ready.

Rescuing food was our thing, but we also did it with style, with panache, with design. And this was because fabulous people started wanting to work with us pro bono. People like Stuart Gregor and Sally Lewis from Liquid Ideas, who helped with our PR and brand, and marketing guru David Nobay, who helped us articulate the core of our purpose, 'To Nourish Our Country'. He then passed us on to designer extraordinaire Vince Frost, who designed our buildings, our logo and our award-winning annual reports. I could not have made this happen. The cause made this happen. It seems that if you do something good, it draws great people, and those people in turn make you look great. That's how it works. OzHarvest is a magnet for magnificent people, so what we do becomes magnificent. It's a beautiful cycle: we are the honey bees that harvest the pollen and nectar, and they are the worker bees that make our honey. It's precious and delicious.

Among my colleagues from my event business days were several chefs, which was handy when starting a food-rescue organisation. I realised very quickly that restaurants don't have much leftover food. Good restaurants are efficient. They run a tight ship; they plan well. Any chef who is taking the time to create beautiful food values their food: what it took to grow it, the time and energy that goes into that process. But when chefs cater external events, there is more opportunity for excess, and they were experiencing the same crazy feeling about throwing away food that I was. And so of course they wanted to support the concept of not wasting food. Asking them to become ambassadors for OzHarvest was a natural way for them to endorse us.

The first chef who completely 'got it' when I was starting OzHarvest was Neil Perry. I was working with him at the time. We have a long history of being behind the scenes together. He catered some crazy, top-end events of mine during RKED, from extravagant birthday parties to corporate gigs. We had fun together. I always let him do whatever he wanted with food, because he is brilliant. He would create fabulous menus, without restraint. He also delivered the finest quality, in everything.

I remember when I'd first arrived back from that trip in Soweto like a woman possessed—I shared with Neil that I was going to start a food-rescue organisation. Shortly after, Neil called me because he had some leftover rice and wanted to do the right thing with it. 'Perfect,' I said, 'I'll be there!' And by the time I arrived, he had made it into a gorgeous stir-fry with some leftover veggies. I could always call on him from then on. He became my go-to guy. When he started Burger Project, until he was able to control the flow of inventory perfectly, he gave us his surplus burgers. Most recently, he blew me away by donating an OzHarvest vehicle and the funds to pay a full-time driver to pick up leftover food from Qantas. He is a generous, creative man and a believer in doing good. He has supported OzHarvest for sixteen years.

Neil brought on his chef mates, and those chefs brought on their mates, to spread the word and join the cause. Among our first ambassadors were Matt Moran, George Calombaris, Peter Gilmore, Guillaume Brahimi, Kumar Mahadevan, Miguel Maestre, Somer Sivrioglu, Colin Fassnidge, Clayton Donovan, Maeve O'Meara and many more—this was before many of them had television profiles. It was extraordinary for us to have their wisdom to draw on. We were disrupting the status quo of the food industry, and chefs were our perfect allies because they were sick and tired of wasting food. They rallied with us because we were doing something tangible about the problem. We recognised them as industry leaders, so we asked for their opinion; few others were asking chefs for their views at that time. Some were beginning to publish bestselling cookbooks, but the celebrity chef phenomenon hadn't yet taken off. There was no *MasterChef*, and no one was involving them in sustainable or charitable events.

My event management skills and my passion started intersecting. I started designing events partnering with our wonderful chefs, where people could experience what we were all about as an organisation. Our CEOCookOff was a perfect example, an annual event that we began in 2011. With this, we turned the table on every gala dinner ever held. We built 50 pop-up kitchens and invited 50 chef ambassadors and CEOs as sous chefs to cook a gourmet sustainable dinner for VIP guests—not the usual dinner guests invited to VIP events, but rather the people we deliver food to in shelters. They are our VIPs. It's a gorgeous sit-down dinner, with live music and entertainment, and table service is provided by our chefs and CEOs! We serve about 1500 people at this dinner event, and we've been doing it for nine years. It has become our major annual fundraiser. Our ambassador chefs, our volunteers, our security staff, our CEOs—everyone—gives so generously of their time. It's an experience of leadership, connection, collaboration and role-modelling. It's about giving yourself a new perspective. It makes invisible people visible. It's both a sight to behold and a heart explosion.

I am continually aware of how the past and the future intersect. My florist life taught me how to bring beauty and artistry to the table. That world led me to my event life, which taught me how to fearlessly create and give people something to take home with them: a feeling, lifelong memories. This all helped to catapult OzHarvest into a brand that has become associated with extraordinary events. And it was through OzHarvest that I learnt how to give people more than just a beautiful memory. They now had the opportunity to walk away with something bigger than themselves. They walk away as part of a movement, a family, a framework for doing good. And so, I always say to people, have no regrets. Your past is relevant. Everything is relevant. From the country you were born in, to what your parents did and didn't teach you, to the part-time job at McDonald's that helped you develop your ability to dream. It's all part of what leads you to who you are and what you stand for. Whether it's your art, your business, your next book or your brand, push nothing away. Embrace it. It's valuable.

# PART 5

# TRUE CALLING

# CHAPTER 34

# TENNIS STRINGS

People often write to me and say they'd really like my help with an idea they'd like to activate. They want to find out how they can achieve something they think I've achieved. If someone goes to the trouble of reaching out to me and asks to meet me, if I can support them in any way, it is my privilege. Working with people who are exploring their lives is fascinating and rewarding, and I always learn something new along the way. I really feel mentoring is incredibly important. I've had some wonderful business mentors along the way, who kindly allowed me to phone them at all hours, and run things past them at times when I felt I needed to brainstorm possibilities or handle difficult situations. It is so nourishing and useful. My friend Rob Kelly, for instance, brings years and years of business experience with him and always has fresh eyes for whatever is going on. He continues to be just a phone call away for me and has been so for more than ten years, even though he lives in London.

Sometimes I feel as though people want to meet me because they saw me or heard me somewhere and suddenly thought, 'I want to start a charity.' They have a deep desire to help people, which is wonderful. If you have an idea for a social problem that isn't being solved—run with it! Don't hesitate! But carefully research the landscape. Check if something similar already exists. There are more than fifty thousand charities in Australia, yet the general public has only heard of around a hundred of them. And then there are thousands more that do good work but are duplicating what other organisations are already doing. To start a new charity that is competing with other, similar charities, just for the sake of it, makes no real sense. I generally suggest checking whether you could use your precious skills to become involved with one that already exists. Maybe your involvement will assist them to do what they do even better. In the business world, competition is part of the game. But a competitive mindset defeats a fundamental part of the intention of the charitable sector.

This sector exists to fill a gap between what government should be doing (but isn't) and what society can do together (with the help of a framework) to assist the vulnerable among us. Charity is that framework. It's the framework of systematically helping each other. The intention of charity is to solve a problem, not to perpetuate it. My dream is that one day OzHarvest will have no more food to collect and no more people to deliver it to, because we'll have figured out as a society how to take care of all our citizens. Our intention is to eventually put ourselves out of business.

From my perspective, charity is a space that should aspire to not exist. It is not a vehicle for becoming a well-known public figure. It might do that, but it would be accidental. It has everything to do with wanting to do something useful and good. Through charity, we are able to figure out how we can make sure people stop falling through the cracks, and alleviate their struggle and pain. We have the resources to take care of our whole society, not just our own little families. So I ask those who come to see me, as Helen from Angel Harvest asked me all those years ago: 'What is your agenda? What is the change you really want to see? What lights you up?'

When people come to me looking for purpose, I sometimes say, maybe there's something you already do every day, or maybe there's something in your life that absolutely irritates you and you wish somebody else would do it or fix it. Maybe that somebody is you. Maybe it's significant enough but nobody has thought of a solution yet. Maybe you haven't got a solution either, but you'd like to have one. Go off and think about it! Give yourself permission not to limit any thought or any silliness. I have found over the years that people's main block is a lack of confidence in themselves and in their idea, and a deep sense of being overwhelmed about where to begin. The simple answer to the latter is, sometimes you just have to begin. In fact, I'd even say there is no beginning, no official beginning at least. There's nothing.

Most people who start something have no real idea where to begin. What can help you begin is knowing it's the right time for you to start. And having the confidence in yourself to know that you radiate the things that the world needs at exactly this point in time, meaning it is the right time. This notion of radiating what the world needs is something I once heard from the teacher and author Ram Dass. It's so true and so beautiful. Your radiance is really the only confidence you need. Your radiance comes through in the things you care about. Sometimes you have to push and shove inside yourself to figure out what that is. Sometimes it's right there in front of you, breaking your heart, just like perfectly wonderful food spilling out of a rubbish bin.

♥

If this book were a mentoring session between you and me, in my office, I would want you to know that what I want most for you is that you find the nobility you are seeking in your life. I want you to experience the purpose you are looking for. I want you to find the beauty that makes it all worthwhile. I want you to know that meaning and nobility can be found in so many different places. Sometimes the process of finding that path is short, sometimes it's long. Sometimes you have to sit in uncertainty for a while and be okay with not knowing. Giving yourself permission to meander with curiosity and not limit your search is so important. If your desire is to serve, then life will grace you with many lessons. It's an incredible exchange.

Do you serve people coffee? Do you work in a post office? At a butcher's shop? A TV station? Do you collect rubbish? Cut hair? Educate children? Represent criminals? Drive buses? Start there. Treat everyone magnificently! Make sure the experience you are giving your colleagues, clients and customers is spectacular. Give them something beyond the money they have paid. Do your job full out! Add value and personal pleasure—and add to your bottom line—by being wonderful, by being generous. Therein lies a great skill in life: to make the best of the situation that has been presented to you. This is where everything converges. This is where your attitude is all. This philosophy has served me well through many years of my life.

But if this feels impossible to you, if you are miserable from Monday to Friday and living for the weekend—that is a clue. Take heed of it. Why does the notion that you could be leaping out of bed seven days a week with joy for what you do feel impossible? Do you believe it's too much to ask? Maybe you've convinced yourself into believing that it's very rare to find that in life. I'm here to tell you there is nothing rare about living that kind of life. When you take rarity out of the equation, you have as much chance of living your best life as not living it. Can you open your imagination to the possibility of living in a way that energises you?

When I was on the kibbutz and was miserable working in the kids' house, I was aware that I was not the right person for that job. Not because I couldn't fulfil the tasks, but because no part of me lit up. The task didn't fulfil me. And the position and the children deserved better than that. It took me some time to find a way to extricate myself, but it's not about the time it takes. If you don't know what it is you want to do, then what matters is to have clarity about what's *not* working for you. Staying in something you don't like for security is an awful trap. Let the clarity of what is not working be the catalyst that pushes you forward. My dissatisfaction pushed me out of that kids' house into accounting, then flower shops, sales and event design. These were things that life put in front of me that were each stepping stones to saying yes to something else, the very stepping stones that led me to my true calling. They were a yes to believing there was something more to what I had to offer. This sense of forward movement changes everything. It's a series of steps in the direction of fully expressing who you are. In the process, you may find you are not as far off the mark as you think.

Many people say 'You can be anything you want to be in this life', but what I know for sure is that it's by truly being yourself, by following your deepest interests, that you can find the greatest fulfilment. You don't have to become more outgoing, bubblier, more like the next person. You don't have to find a grandiose cause. It can be something right in front of you. To make OzHarvest happen, I see now that what I did was simply let myself become more myself. Nobody ever told me during my childhood that I had gifts. But you know what? Today, I know I have a gift. I must have, because people are inspired to give me their time, their money, their buildings, to do the work that I do. And I believe this happens just by being yourself. By being present, by being in alignment with your joy, your excitement, by knowing what lights you up. These traits are very compelling to be around. Your 'lit-up-ness' ignites others. It's an energy, a current. Tapping in to what delights you will lead you to a place that perhaps you can only imagine right now. It's what you dream of, sometimes without even knowing it. The gifts you require for your calling will meet you there. They will appear, reveal themselves, and catch you on wings you didn't know existed.

A couple of years ago, a woman called Monica came to my office for a mentoring session because she was desperate—in her words—to find her purpose. She sat down and said to me, 'There is something missing in my daily life and I don't know where to find it.' I said, 'Well, tell me a little bit about yourself. Tell me a little bit about your life. Share with me anything you think is important for me to guide you.' She answered that she had kids and was doing a job she didn't love. In her words, 'It's not what I want to be doing forever. I don't love it but it's fine. It's money.'

'Do you find it stimulating in any way? Do you like the people?' I asked. I was trying to find any nuggets that I could mine. I was listening for clues she may inadvertently drop about her deepest interests. She used the word 'dull', and it sounded like she thought everyone else's life was much more exciting and fulfilling. She didn't feel as though she was as productive as she could be.

'Monica. It sounds like you're just making do. Just living for bread. It reminds me of a beautiful story, a Yiddish story that I grew up with.' And I started to share with her this tale.

'There was once a man who had been looking for work for weeks on end. It was the time of the Great Depression and his wife and children were starving. With this heavy burden upon him, he heads out on yet another day, desperate to try to find work, any work, and once again his efforts are thwarted. He walks home. His heart is anguished, his feet are dragging. Another failed day of no work, no money and no food. How will he face his family? All of a sudden, lo and behold, right there in front of him he finds a shiny silver shekel. He picks it up in disbelief and with complete and utter glee and joy he runs straight to the closest bakery and asks them to give him all the bread he can buy with half a shekel. And after that, he runs to the flower seller on the corner and asks for the biggest bunch of flowers his remaining half-shekel will buy. With his arms laden, he hops, skips and jumps all the way home. He knocks on his front door and when it opens, there stands his wife with their six children. 'I found some money!' he cries out. The children are already tearing into the bags of bread and eating it with relish to feed their starving bellies. But when his wife sees the flowers, she starts shrieking. 'Are you crazy?' she yells. 'You find some money and you don't spend it all on food? We are starving and you waste it on flowers? What were you thinking? What could have gone through your head?' He looks at her and in a quiet voice he says, 'My dearest, the bread is in order for us all to survive. But the flowers are to make our lives worth living.'

I looked straight into Monica's face. She was pensive. 'Monica, I think what you want to find is the flowers. Is that right?' She nodded her head.

'Tell me, is there something particular on your agenda that you want to achieve by finding your purpose?'

'Yes,' she said. 'I want to feel good. I want to do something useful. I want to make a difference.'

I could hear a genuine quest going on within her. Then I said to her, 'Monica, what do you love doing most in the whole world? Don't limit yourself. It doesn't have to be about work. It can be as left of field as you want it to be. But think hard and dig deep. Close your eyes if you have to.'

She didn't need any time. Suddenly, she lit up. Literally. She said, 'This is going to sound weird but I LOVE TENNIS!' I was a little taken aback. It was so obscure.

I said, 'Okay! Which part of tennis? Tell me about that! Do you play?'

'No. I go to the Australian Open' she said. 'My children are ball catchers. I watch it incessantly on TV. I just love to watch it. And I volunteer at a couple of tennis clubs.'

I could see she just loved this sport. And then she said, 'Now that I'm talking about it, lately when I'm watching those matches, I see the tennis players, especially the top players, use so many rackets. They restring the rackets, but I've been wondering what happens to the old tennis strings. It's piles and piles of synthetic stuff and natural fibres dumped into landfill. Surely they are valuable. They've been used by these famous tennis players . . .'

My environmental and sustainability lamps lit up. 'Monica, if you already love tennis, and you've started worrying about those strings, have you found out if anybody is repurposing or recycling them?'

She looked at me. 'Oh my God, I've never thought about that. I could check that out at the clubs I work at.'

I said, 'Great! Your homework is to find out what happens to those discarded tennis strings. If all tennis players discard them, there must be graveyards full of old strings somewhere. What else could they be used for? In Africa, old telephone wires are used to make incredible artisanal baskets and objects of beauty. Perhaps strings could be useful in some way. Call me if you want to see me again. But I think you know what to do.' She jumped out of her chair like a woman possessed and off she went.

Six weeks later Monica waltzed in to my office. 'Here's what's happened in the last six weeks,' she said. 'I'm so excited. I connected with a tennis centre and discovered they were very excited to see what I could do with those strings. Then I connected with an arts centre and they suggested they could use the strings for one of their upcoming fundraiser art exhibitions.' I was thrilled for her. It was all going so well.

Monica's story stands out to me because it is proof that you can have a hobby that lights you up that you don't even realise can turn into a passion project. In this case, a very sustainable one! In no way does it have to be traditional. It can be as obscure as tennis strings! There is no formula. The only prerequisite is that it has to light you up. Her discovery had lit me up too.

But wait. There's more to Monica's story. Six weeks after that meeting, she came back. 'How is everything?' I asked. She was angry this time. Upset.

'You won't believe it. The arts centre I contacted has planned to have this amazing exhibition and I'm not included at all!'

'Tell me what you did for the arts centre?' I asked.

'I suggested they use the strings,' she said.

'So, you collected the strings from the tennis centre and took them to the arts centre?'

'No,' she said, 'I simply arranged to have the strings assembled by the local tennis club and told the arts centre they'd need to collect them.'

'What part did you have in setting it up then?' I asked.

'Nothing, really,' she said. 'But they should have included me. It was my idea.'

'On what basis should they have included you? You didn't get them the strings. You didn't deliver them personally. You didn't check out their space. You planted the seed of an idea, but you didn't follow through with it. Can you see that you didn't add value beyond having the idea?'

She fell silent and I could see she suddenly realised her desire to be recognised had taken over. She realised that having an idea wasn't the same as manifesting that idea.

'Monica,' I said. 'You did a beautiful thing. You wanted tennis strings to be saved and they were. Instead of worrying about how you weren't involved, consider how you could do more of this. How do you scale up this idea? How can you stay in a lit-up place around rescuing tennis strings? Remember I asked you what was your agenda? What do you think your agenda is now?'

She said, 'I think I need to go home and think about it. I've learnt something today.' She knew what I was implying. It was a confronting but powerful moment for us. I could see that she was ready to serve (excuse the pun) her ideas in a different way now, and that would eventually lead her to ask the question, *What does the world need from me?*

# CHAPTER 35

# SILVER VIXEN

In 2006, I married Irving, a beautiful man who I believed would be my (third) one and only, forever. For a number of years we were beautifully connected and interwoven. He was intelligent. He was ethical. He was kind, and I loved how he took care of his teenage daughter. All these qualities were so attractive to me. Unfortunately, after eight years of harmony, irreconcilable differences began to take over our lives. Our distancing was a slow, slow burn. One of the straws that finally broke the camel's back had to do with my hair. The very hair that once made me visible to the world, when I had my incredible perm, was also the hair that made me totally invisible to my husband.

I'd been streaking my hair, highlighting it, dyeing it dark brown, blonde, red for so long that I barely knew what my natural colour really was. I knew there was some—God forbid—age creeping through, but it was always magically covered up in a jiffy. The upkeep was intense, but I kept doing it. I didn't question it at first; it was fairly easy, even though it was a big expense every couple of weeks. But after some years, I found I couldn't afford the time anymore. Each visit meant hours and hours at the hairdresser.

Then, one day, I was filmed for a beautiful OzHarvest short film that we produced. It was gorgeous. But in one section they had filmed me from the back, and I noticed this round circular patch of white hair on the top of my head, like a little hat. I was appalled. I thought, *What's a nice Jewish girl like me doing looking like the Pope?* I felt vain, but I loathed it so much. I could no longer hide how quickly my roots were growing. I had to fix this.

Now previously, I'd asked a few hairdressers if I could go natural—whatever that was—and each one had said, 'No bloody way!' They said, 'You're too young! You just can't do it.' No one was eager to change my status to 'old' in the eyes of the world at the age of sixty-two. Then one day, I found a hairdresser who did not say no. Alison Schore was recommended to me as a virtuoso of colouring hair. She was an expert, so I knew I was in good hands. At the time I met her, she worked from her beautiful little home salon. I walked in, exasperated, and said, 'Alison, what am I going to do? I cannot dye my hair anymore. The upkeep is beyond me!' I waited for the opposition, but it didn't come. Maybe I secretly wanted it to come, but it just didn't. Instead, she said, 'Okay, no probs!' And before I had a chance to change my mind, she sat me down, slapped stuff on my head and bleached all the colour out to allow the natural hue to take over. When I stood up and looked in the mirror, well, I almost died. I thought, *Oh my God, is this who I really am? And now I have to be fully accepted for who I am.* It was scary, even a touch sickening. But at the same time, underneath the panic, I felt a strange power creeping in. It felt surprisingly authentic, standing there, in my naked truth. I could hardly believe it. My hair was practically OzHarvest bright yellow because of the bleach, though this was only transitional. (I wish I'd thought to turn my head into an OzHarvest installation, but in the shock of the moment that artistry escaped me!)

When I arrived home, I walked into our apartment and saw my husband standing in the kitchen. He looked up at me. I said, 'Don't panic, it's still me! It's just me. All I've done is taken the colour out and cut my hair.' He was utterly speechless. He was in major shock, to say the very least. Now it's true, I knew he loved brunettes and he loved long hair. And it's not like he was prepared for this, it's not as if I had told him I was going to be doing this. But I hadn't told him because I hadn't known I was doing it that day! I thought I'd go in to have a consultation with a hairdresser, and that perhaps it would begin this big process for some later date. But she did it! On the spot. And here I was, in all my vulnerable glory.

He looked absolutely horrified. It was pretty confronting how he was looking at me. All he could muster was. 'What. Have. You. Done? I don't like this.' I could not help but stare at his bald head and see the irony. In blatant self-defence I said, 'Listen, I wish you had hair. Any colour hair. I love luscious hair! But there's not much you can do about your baldness, is there? Can you love me as I am?' He just stood there, glaring. I stood there. It was a white-hair bald-head stand-off. It would have been absolutely tragic if it weren't so funny.

As a 62-year-old woman I felt I did not have to ask permission for anything about my own body, but I also never imagined I would be judged so harshly for something like this. I honestly thought that by this point in my life, my partner wouldn't be judging me for my looks. I assumed everyone loved me for who I was. And in my innocence, I assumed I would be even more beautiful in my natural state—even if my natural state was currently OzHarvest yellow! I admit, I wasn't looking great. But even as the weeks and months moved on and my hair started relaxing and becoming silver and stylish, nothing changed. He truly struggled. It turns out he thought it was the most shocking thing he had ever seen. The weird thing is, I don't believe he ever got over it. I'd become invisible to him. There was no turning back.

It definitely took time for me to get used to how I looked with my new hair. As it transitioned into its natural glory, it was not salt and pepper as I had initially thought. There was no pepper. I was only salt. I was pure white and I embraced it. But it wasn't exactly easy to feel sexy when my husband didn't want to come near me. And my sisters didn't love it. It took a while for them to come around. They initially felt I looked 'so old'. And it really sucked when people started stopping me on the street, completely starstruck, thinking I was the real-life flesh-and-blood Iris Apfel (who is awesome), but who is in fact 98 years old! I mean, seriously, couldn't they have at least thought I was her daughter? But once my ego got over the fact that I might have looked like I was in my nineties to some, I was actually thrilled that I never again had to cover my hair with chemicals. It was just a new look to me, but it turns out it was surprisingly controversial. Although I was fine to be perceived as the age I was, my age was not the issue. I had to come to terms with the fact that as a woman, letting myself age visibly was quite confronting to the wider society. I'd had no idea what my practical hair decision would unleash.

The natural process of ageing, for women (and for some men too), has been subverted in our minds through our social conditioning. People called me 'brave', as though letting myself be officially my age in the eyes of the world was an absolutely out-there concept. It's so fascinating that as a man you turn into a 'silver fox' as you age: an attractive, charming and classy middle-aged grey-haired male. Think about it. George Clooney, Colin Firth, Pierce Brosnan, Daniel Day-Lewis, Hugh Grant, Jon Bon Jovi—all getting better with age. No one called them brave. Not to mention my all-time heart-throb Richard Gere. He only became more beautiful in my eyes—and he was 40 and very grey in *Pretty Woman!* I wish I could have become a silver vixen in my husband's eyes (or anybody's eyes for that matter; it may still happen). But mostly, I'm determined to look in the mirror and see myself as attractive and charming and classy. If I don't change the narrative within myself, then who will?

If I wasn't already a social activist around sustainability, maybe I'd be standing for women to proudly embrace their wrinkles and white hair. But I have to pick my battles. I do have an opportunity, however, to see how ageing plays out in ways that are beyond skin deep. So many people come into my office saying, 'Ah, if only I'd done this or that when I was young. I'm too old now.' Why is age so often the barrier when it comes to fulfilling our true calling? The only real battle anyone has to fight when it comes to ageing is the battle within themselves. Society makes that difficult for us. But ultimately, the choice is ours. And the real question is, do we have the courage to be seen as we are and follow our calling, regardless of how society has brainwashed (or hair washed) us to see ourselves?

So, ironically, for the second time in my life, my hair had created alchemy. I felt a deep emancipation, one I didn't even know I needed. I had shed something and gained immense freedom to stand proudly as who I was without shame. I was older, yes, and yet somehow I felt I had even more wisdom to share with the world.

Uncovering my real hair inadvertently uncovered the heartbreak in my marriage. Sadly, within a year, our marriage ended. These days, people stop me on the street to ask me what gorgeous colour I've put in my hair. I've started saying, 'It's God's colour!'

# CHAPTER 36

# YESTERDAY, TODAY, TOMORROW

Recently, I was walking along the beach when a woman came up to me and said, 'I know you're walking and I don't want to interrupt you, but I love what you do and I'm waiting for the day when I can do that too!'

I looked at her and said, 'Why wait? Why not do it now?'

She just looked at me and said, 'Oh. I work.'

'Uh-huh,' I said. We smiled at each other, had a bit more chit chat, then we parted ways.

Another person stopped me on the street yesterday. He was so excited he almost yelled, 'I've just retired! I'm going to do what you do: something in the charity world. I have an idea!'

'That's great!' I said. 'What are you waiting for?'

'Well, I'm going to go on holidays first.'

'Uh-huh,' I said. We waved at each other, and walked on.

Growing up, I watched my mother scrimp and save for when she could live really well, for the time when she retired. She was planning, planning, planning, so she would have this backup. She was coming from a mindset that thinks you have to save and save because something might happen, and you will be left poor or in trouble or in need. And then when I was 26 years old, she became ill and died two years later at the age of 63. The reality of this experience was a huge jolt for me, because she'd planned to live a very full life, once she could 'afford' to do so. Rich in experience. And all that living in scarcity, and saving for another time, a time of abundance, another future, it never happened. She lived that way for nothing. She was never unhappy, nor did she ever seem as though she was challenged by her choices. But her practicality won the day. The day she died, I thought, *What was the point of all her scrimping and saving?* It wasn't her planning for her future that I found problematic. It was all the compromises she must have made along the way, compromises that steered her away from the real gifts of her soul, from her real joy. That day I decided to live my life differently. I broke free from the hold she'd unintentionally placed on me, in relation to living in a space of deficiency. It was the beginning of my understanding that abundance has nothing to do with being financially secure, it is about emotional freedom.

In 2009, my son Edo met the woman he knew he would marry, Jo, and a few years later they did marry. Much like me in my younger years, Jo had followed a life of doing the things she'd been told were sensible. For instance, she found a job in the corporate sector after leaving university, even though that was not what she really wanted. She had internalised that same message I had—steer away from your soul gifts, plan for security and practicality. Very soon, she was earning well, succeeding enormously, yet working herself to the bone and feeling growing anxiety and stress. It did not make her happy. Even though she was really good at her job and it was a very safe path for her, it came at a cost. And then she met Edo, a musician, and their relationship steered her back to the truth of what lit up her world: music.

She and Edo became a musical duo, travelling the world sharing their songs. Initially, it was not easy to give up all that money and the clear trajectory of the corporate ladder. The uncertain life of an artist was not totally natural to her. But she had incredible gifts, and once she allowed them to flow freely, the music they created moved people deeply. So she bravely shifted her life to exactly where it needed to be. Before she knew it, their music career began to provide a comfortable living, while she was doing exactly what she wanted to do. She was living her bliss. It was a vision of beauty to witness her joy and energy.

It's hard to write about this, but on 21 July 2015, Jo was diagnosed with cancer. Before we even had time to fully process the news, on 21 September—exactly two months later—she died. She was 36 years old. We barely knew what hit us. It was very painful. It still is. Our beautiful Jo was gone from our midst, and my son was now a widower. It was surreal and I'm still in shock that it even happened. But one thing is for sure: Jo died with such grace and acceptance. She was a gift to us. And she had lived exactly how she'd wanted to live during those last years. Even though she had dreams of doing so much more, even though she wanted to continue to live, she knew she had honoured her deepest calling. She had lived a life immersed in the deep satisfaction of work that was meaningful to her, and she left us with her sublime songs.

We all know that tragedies happen, but collectively we seem to be convinced that tragedies happen to other people. No one is immune to becoming those 'other people'. Many of us do what we can to prevent death. We take care of ourselves and stay healthy, but the truth is that nobody knows when they are going to die. We can plan and plot and control and manage, but, ultimately, we are not in control. These days, when people ask me about my plans in two years, in one year, in one month, I cannot help but be completely aware of the fact that I may not be around then. In fact, I can't even be sure I'll be around to see the publication of this book. When Jo's death happened, my sense of perspective changed. It may sound morbid, but I think being aware of death has helped me tremendously to live a better life. A life where I wake up aware and grateful that today I have an opportunity to use my precious energy, to experience everything in all its technicoloured glory, to be grateful for every precious relationship and to be present in the precious moment of now.

Often, when I arrive home at the end of my day, it feels like a thousand people have said to me, 'One day—when I pay off my mortgage, when my kids have grown up, when I don't have to pay school fees anymore, when I don't have to look after my mother, when I can afford it—I will live the life that I've always wanted to live.' And yes, maybe the stars have to align, and yes, maybe all in good time, and yes, maybe you are only ready when you are ready. But if there is one thing I know, it's this: there may not be a 'one day'. That time you are waiting for may never come. My mother's death, and more especially Jo's death, were each tremendously personal examples of the imperative to act now. If you have the awareness of this, reward yourself with the pleasure of not putting anything off for another day.

If you have already decided what you want to share with the world, I promise you that you can start that today, in big and small ways. If you want to do something, want it *now*, because tomorrow is not guaranteed. It may mean stepping out of your comfort zone, doing something you've never done before—as I did—or it may simply mean gliding into something that makes you incredibly happy, something you have never given yourself permission to do before. Whatever it is, doing it is a powerful moment, and today is a powerful day.

And the woman on the beach, and the man on the street? What were they really waiting for? Maybe they are now doing exactly what they planned to do—I hope so. Or maybe they are still waiting for that 'perfect moment'. The truth is that at work, on holidays or wherever you may be, your sacred moment, to do exactly what you've always wanted to do, can be and is now. It doesn't begin when you start your charity; it doesn't begin after your overseas trip. It is alive in your actions now. There is no other day to begin.

# CHAPTER 37

# HEARING THE UNHEARD

There is an old African parable that I love, and it goes something like this. A tribal leader from a village deep in the heart of Africa wanted his son to learn the basics of being a good leader, so he called on the wise master of the tribe to instruct the boy. When the son arrived at the master's hut, the master sent him into the jungle with the instruction to return to the tribe in one year. His mission: to describe to them the sound of the jungle. A year later, when the boy returned, he was asked to describe all he had heard. The boy said, 'Master, I could hear the leaves rustle, the birds hum, the crickets chirp, the grass blow, the bees buzz and the wind whisper and holler.' When the boy finished sharing all he had heard, the master said, 'Go back into the jungle, my boy, and listen to what else you can hear.' The boy was puzzled by this request. He was sure he had heard every single sound already. For days and nights on end the young boy sat once again, alone in the jungle, listening. But the only sounds he heard were the ones he had heard already. Then one morning, as he sat silently beneath the trees, he started to discern faint sounds unlike those he had heard before. The more acutely he listened, the clearer the sounds became. The boy was filled with awe. 'These must be the sounds the master wanted me to hear,' he reflected. The boy ran back to the village, and went straight to the master. The master asked him, 'What did you hear, my boy?' 'Master,' he replied reverently, 'when I listened most closely, I could hear the unheard. The sound of flowers opening. The sound of the sun warming the earth. The sound of the grass drinking the morning dew.' The master smiled and nodded approvingly. 'To hear the unheard is the necessary discipline to be a good ruler. For only when a ruler has learnt to listen closely to people's hearts, hearing their uncommunicated feelings, their unexpressed pains and their unspoken complaints, can he hope to inspire confidence in his people, and meet the true needs of his citizens.'

There are a million books devoted to the attributes that make a great leader. I started reading these types of book some years ago, and found very powerful ones that have served me well. There is so much to learn, and to be reinforced, always. But when I first started OzHarvest, it didn't occur to me to read a leadership book, because I had no plan or intention of leading people. I was too busy rescuing food and 'doing'. I didn't know then that I was building a movement. Maybe if I'd read a lot in preparation for starting OzHarvest, I would have been paralysed with fear, or completely overwhelmed. But, looking back, I built OzHarvest without knowing leadership was a 'thing'. I freewheeled it for over a decade! I learnt all the basics on the job, and experience often teaches you through your mistakes. What not to do is also a good teacher.

It's actually taken me a long time to even see myself as a leader. I was comfortable with leading—that bit has come quite naturally. But being called a leader is a whole other thing to get your head around. I think becoming a leader is a gradual process. It takes time to own it and to live it. I only really realised I was in the business of being a leader when I was guided by my mentors to build a management team at OzHarvest. This team would walk into my office saying, 'Hey, boss!' Initially, it totally freaked me out, as well as making me giggle on the inside. Me? I'd honestly be almost looking over my shoulder to see who this 'boss' they were referring to might be! Until that moment, I'd simply been doing what needed to be done and taking responsibility for those actions. If my staff came to me with a problem, I'd go into solving and fixing mode. My fix-it default mode has not done me any favours in my marriages. But in a business context, I always found it quite helpful. OzHarvest fixes a problem. I love that.

Having a management team to share the load has led to considerable personal growth for me, and has benefited OzHarvest. It meant I had to learn to delegate and trust people, good people I had chosen not only for their skills but also for their integrity. Trust is a huge part of leadership, and it takes time to build. But trust is also the foundation of building a team.

I came to realise that OzHarvest had grown so much, and I couldn't just continue solving things on my own. It wasn't sustainable or effective for OzHarvest or for me. Today, when people come to me with a problem, I know it is my job to listen, to be present, to not talk too much or 'fix'. That may be obvious to others, but it was not the way I operated in the past. Now I know that when I'm not being the best listener, I'm not being the best leader. The whole thing about 'leadership' is about working it out together. These days I listen to what my people think, and we give each other permission to share and be heard. I have found this to be such an enjoyable way to communicate. I had to learn this, and am continuing to learn these skills.

It may appear that the work I do is about impacting things 'out there' in the world, in our society. And it is. But actually, I have the most direct impact upon the people who work with me. They love to have the opportunity to participate in a value-driven life. They love being part of something that feels so good. It is my job to nurture and upskill my people—even though that means they will probably leave the nest! Other companies will want them and offer them jobs they can't refuse. Yet I'd rather take that risk than not have them grow. Guiding them to become the best they can be is a big part of my role. Guiding them to do things they didn't think they could do, or ways of being that they hadn't considered part of their skill set is a very exhilarating process. This creates leaders. That is what working in and around OzHarvest is about. I can't believe that for so long I thought it was about making all the decisions and solving every-thing. It's not, and I'm so glad it's not. The rewards of collaboration are beautiful. This is part of the beauty of leadership.

Having said that, as much as you are a team, when the proverbial muck does hit the fan, as it sometimes does, it will always be on you, as a leader. It comes very naturally to want to pass the buck. Suffering the loneliness of leadership is not easy, but comes with the role—which is why mentors and books help so much. You can't say, 'I knew nothing about this or that issue; it's that person's fault.' It doesn't work that way. It might have occurred in someone else's department, but who is ultimately responsible for that department? If a tyre falls off a vehicle at OzHarvest and someone gets hurt, I am responsible. It's my finger on the pulse. It's my understanding of the business. If I am responsible for something, I am responsible, period.

Being willing to roll up your sleeves and do whatever needs to be done, no matter the task, is the kind of authentic leadership that sets the tone for the culture of an organisation. Nothing can be beneath a leader. Nothing. I live by that. Some of our current business and global leaders seem to be steeped in self-centredness; it's at the core of the way they lead. They pick and choose what they take responsibility for. They misuse their power. There is no sustainable movement forward for our world when leaders engage in corruption and environmental carnage. And make no mistake, the misuse of power can sometimes be subtle, and examining this concept is key for all of us. Where does our power lie?

A leader who misuses power is a leader by name only. There is no good action in that, there is no future in that. The real question a leader must ask is, *Is this action good for the community? For the nation? For children? For the planet? Is this respectful? Does it celebrate and acknowledge our diversity? Does this create more fear in the world or more love?* This is why I love the African parable, because leading requires perception beyond just the senses. It means we are having to listen in a way that involves more than our ears. We listen with our hearts.

We listen with our humanity. We pre-empt the needs of those around us, of the world around us. Sometimes it simply means knowing how to ask the right questions and implementing wise action. This kind of listening is our sacred duty as leaders.

Perhaps you are reading this and thinking, 'I'm not a leader in my work or my life, so this doesn't apply to me.' I read a book once—*The Monk Who Sold His Ferrari* by Robin Sharma—that talks about how we are all leaders without titles. It really stuck, and I often pass that piece of wisdom on to people because it speaks to the heart of this matter. All of us are leading, all the time. Whether you are an employee in an office, or the boss of a charity, or at home with your kids or your neighbours or your partner, what you do matters. How you do it matters. People are watching, learning, remembering and understanding the world in relation to you, through you. We all have an opportunity to be the best we can be, to be an example of the best we have to offer. It applies to everyone in every place, even when we want to put the responsibility of skilful action into the hands of other people; even when we are, in fact, in the hands of other people. It can be confronting, but when it comes down to it, with or without a title, you are a leader. Own it. The buck stops with you.

# CHAPTER 38

# ONE LITTLE STARFISH

Around 2006, I met someone who fundamentally changed my life. My first OzHarvest logistics person, Tom Sawkins, said to me one day, 'There's this man out there doing extraordinary work. He's a retired Salvation Army officer who is still doing incredible things off his own bat. He still feeds people.' Instantly I said, 'I want to meet him.'

Not long afterwards, Tom brought this man to our tiny little office and said, 'Ronni, meet Hilton Harmer.' And there he was—Hilton—in his pristine Salvation Army officer uniform, with eyes so blue and so beautiful that they took me aback.

'I feed a lot of people,' he said.

'Tell me more,' I replied.

It turns out he was going from boarding house to boarding house (low-income rental housing), of his own volition, to feed the people he could, with the food he could find. There was something in his spirit that just felt so real. As he spoke to me, I instantly knew that I could trust this man to do anything. Giving him food for his boarding-house run was not within the model of how we operated. We deliver to registered charitable agencies. He wasn't an agency. He wasn't a charity. He was a one-man show. But I could tell he was the real deal. I said, 'Tom, please give Hilton whatever he needs.'

It was an honour to go rogue with Hilton. There was no way we could pass up that opportunity. His work was too exceptional. Every Tuesday, from that day forth, he started coming to OzHarvest, we'd load up his truck, and then one of us would go with him on his run. I'd go sometimes. We'd drive to a boarding house—often in a suburb you'd never expect. He'd call someone in advance, to tell them we were rocking up. On arrival, he'd open his doors, his old ghetto blaster would go up on the roof of his van, belting out tunes, while we unloaded boxes of beautiful food and put it in rows on the sidewalk. People would cluster around with so much excitement. It was a weekly treat of food and connection. We were the charity equivalent of an ice-cream truck. We made people happy. It was a marvellous, incredible experience to witness the magic of giving. It was so real. It was one-on-one contact with the most amazing people who were otherwise disenfranchised and completely hidden from mainstream society.

The irony of these boarding houses is that although the occupants are packed together in their small living quarters, many are completely isolated, alone in their rooms, all day, every day. Hilton's visits brought hope and social contact. Food was the connector. And I was able to watch Hilton's magic. He had an ability to ease their anxieties, with food and with kind words. It improved their mental health and their physical health in that moment. Hilton had a relationship with everybody. He was strong, he'd call it how it was. He'd laugh at things that might offend someone else. His giving had no strings attached. Everyone could be who they were.

There was a time when people would call me and say, 'I've just walked past this homeless person on the street and I think they need help.' I barely ever knew what to do. So I'd call Hilton. I'd say, 'Hilton, on the corner of this and this street there's a person who needs help.' And he'd say, 'Okay, I'm on it, Ronni.' And he'd pick them up in his truck and put them in a motel. To this day, he says OzHarvest helps him do the work he does. But I just think of how much more we could do to help him help others. His fundamental belief about his life is that he is here to serve. He taught me more things than I ever learnt in school or university. I don't know if he knows that. He taught me simply through the way he lives and breathes, and the same goes for his beautiful wife Joyce. It's very simple and profound. I am so indebted, beyond grateful to know them.

Reflecting on my life and OzHarvest as I write this book led me to want to visit Hilton. He's a touchstone for me. He reminds me of things I need to remember. It's not often we have time to just sit together. We set up a date and the day comes around. It's a boiling hot day and I've just landed from Adelaide, and I'm already half an hour late. As I pull up into his street, I see him, ready, anxiously waiting for me on the sidewalk outside his house, in his Salvation Army T-shirt. He greets me warmly, escorts me from my car to his exquisite garden, where a table is set in the shade with drinks and treats and metal hearts on a string that he has hung from a tree just for this meeting, just for me. That's him to a tee. Beauty in the details.

'I put those hearts there because I was so excited about today,' he tells me. 'I prayed about this little gathering. That we would feel God's presence. It had to be hearts on that tree because of what OzHarvest is all about, the number of people I see going out that gate of mine with arms full of food who never would have had that, who . . .' His voice cracks, and he loses his words. My eyes fall on the centrepiece of the table, an oversized box of tissues.

'I put those there,' he says, 'because I thought, who am I kidding? Ronni and I are never going to get through a cup of tea without cryin'!' We laugh, and cry a little through our laughter. We always talk from the heart. He's well prepared for that.

I sit down and help myself to a cold drink. I'm so glad to be here. To stop 'all the busy' for a moment, and come to ground with my friend. But there is no way I'm going to talk about my busy. Hilton is 80 years old and is probably busier than anyone I know. 'I'm as busy as a one-legged tap dancer,' he often says, making me laugh. Hilton works twelve to fifteen hours a day, every single day. His job is helping people, any people, and he's been doing it for 57 years. I grab my phone, go to voice memos and press record. I know I'm going to want to remember this conversation.

'How do you do it, Hilton? How do you still have the strength?' I ask.

'Ronni, the day will come when I have to give this up. It will become too demanding. These days I'm finding it harder to do what I gotta do. I'm getting old. I got the heart and the mind, but I don't have the body anymore. But regardless, I never wake up feeling it's a burden to face the day. I know I'm going to help someone this day, you know? I can't wait for that. But sometimes in the morning, I sit on the side of my bed, and I don't feel like getting up, you know? I just put my hands up in the air and I say, "Please God, help me. Help me to help someone today." And I just get up. And when I'm halfway through the day I realise I'm not tired at all. Then by the time I get home, I can hardly walk. But just before I roll into bed, I thank God that we have come through another day together. I always say, "Thank you, God, we did it again." And then I say, "Thank you for my bed." I always say that. Because some people don't have a bed, you know?'

At the time of writing this, Hilton helps 70 families a week. He drops off OzHarvest food to them, or they come to his home, where he lines things up on his lawn and people help themselves. That is only a portion of what he does.

'It's never-ending, Ronni,' he tells me. 'There is a never-ending need. People, people everywhere, far too many for a person my age to reach. Even when I take my shoes off at night, I know there are other people I could be helping. I've never reached that point where I can say, "Oh, isn't that good, there's no one else to help." Never. It's unbelievable in this country that people know starvation. But they do. You tell that to some people in this country and they wouldn't believe you. They'd say, "How could that possibly be?" But it's everywhere.'

It is overwhelming. All the need. All the suburbs and homes of people that most of us don't see and never will see. I feel a tightening in my chest just thinking about it. 'Do you get overwhelmed, Hilton? Is it ever just too much for you?'

'Ronni,' he says, 'to stop me from being overwhelmed, I think of the story of the boy who was on a beach where millions of starfish had been washed up. He was walking along picking them up one and a time, and a cynic said to the boy, "Why are you wasting your time? You'll never be able to help all those starfish!" And the boy said, "Maybe not, but I've helped the ones I've thrown back in the water!" And Ronni, that's how I approach what I do. Sure, I can't help them all. But I can help the ones I interact with. And while it's not front-page activity, I know it makes a difference. And to me, that's what life is about!'

Difference, indeed. The tissues are certainly being used. I can see his body is tired, but he is so energised at the same time. I ask him about that energy, those values. I've never asked him about his upbringing before. He tells me that his values came from his mum and dad. 'It's a bit hard not to devote your life to service when you have it modelled in your house, morning, noon and night. My parents were Salvation Army but not officers. When I became an officer, I was paid to be good. But they were good for nothing!' We laugh. He has a great laugh. I try to imagine a little boy Hilton. I can see the boy in his face, maybe a freckly, Aussie kid.

'They had a little property outside Gympie, in South Queensland,' he continues. 'My dad had a veggie garden. He had cows and chickens. You would never come to our place without leaving with something. You'd leave with some eggs, or you'd leave with some carrots or potatoes or lettuce, or a jug of milk or something. Butter that my mum made. Morning, noon and night, my mother and father were the most beautiful people. My parents taught me love for other people. They had real Christian values.'

The word 'Christian' jolts me somehow. It makes me imagine his Jesus-loving home in rural South Queensland, and me all the way in apartheid South Africa in my Jewish house with Florrie and our other live-in staff. We probably had the most different sorts of upbringing you could imagine. And then, almost like he's read my mind, he says, 'When I went to school, the kids from the Catholic school would sing, "Protestant, Protestant, go to hell," and we'd sing, "Catholic dogs, stink like frogs, in and out of all the logs." That used to go on day after day, coming home from school. Or if your daughter or your son happened to start courting a Catholic, my God, it was a national crisis back in those days. Now there is slightly more acceptance in the world. Slightly. We are slowly realising if we don't accept each other, we are shooting ourselves in the foot. Anybody who is doing something to create better values in the world should be embraced. We are too quick to see differences.

'A Buddhist nun once said to me, "It seems to me that we are all little creeks, running into the one big river." Isn't that beautiful? Isn't that the most beautiful expression?'

'That's so beautiful,' I say. It could not be truer in this moment, Christian and Jew, in this suburban Garden of Eden of Hilton's creation. Such perfect harmony.

'I've been obsessed with my desire to "lighten the load" of my fellow travellers in this world for a long time, Ronni, regardless of the inconveniences it may require. My son says, "You're a rescuer, Dad, it's not helpful to rescue people." But I don't agree with that. I don't do what other people can do for themselves. But sometimes there has got to be someone to get you on the first rung of the ladder, or you'll never get there. There are four very necessary things in life: air, water, food and accommodation. Universally, they are life's essentials. And sometimes I think, "You gotta rescue some people." There are some really bad situations out there. People are so happy with the food I give them sometimes, you'd think I'd given them a bar of gold!'

And with that, we start talking about the meaning of our lives. I'm thinking about purpose. About repurpose. About what that means. Purpose is a word I use a lot now in my talks, yet it's becoming increasingly challenging to use. As it's emerged into the mainstream, its true value is getting somewhat lost. One thing I've discovered is that purpose is not something 'out there'. It's not something you can find only after you've understood something, finished something or found something. True purpose can't be packaged up and put on a supermarket shelf for you to buy from a person, company or brand.

'What's your purpose, Hilton?' I ask, as I bite into a sausage roll. 'Do we all need purpose? Do we look for it or does it find us?' I sort of know what he might answer, but maybe I don't. I want his wisdom to carry me, somehow.

'I back off from purpose and meaning, Ronni,' he says. 'I don't want to be preachy. I just leave it to each individual's intelligence. You can remain selfish for the rest of your life, I suppose. But I like to think that people, anybody, that I have helped might think, "Gee, that was nice, I'd really like to do the same for someone else." One good thing begets another,' Hilton says. 'Good work draws goodwill like a magnet will draw metal.'

'That's exactly how OzHarvest works,' I say. 'That's exactly how this whole thing began for me, and how it continues!'

'Yes, because people want to help someone who is actually doing something,' he replies. 'My purpose is to try to make a difference in people's lives. But not make a big deal of it. Any time I step outside my house, just in my yard, I'm on high alert. Anyone could need something. To make a difference, it starts at home. I'm a hypocrite if I don't make a difference to Joyce, my wife, first. And then to my Muslim neighbours to my right, and my Greek neighbours to my left. It's a ripple effect. It ripples out from home. I like getting to know my neighbours. Sometimes they don't really want to know me. That's okay. But if they want to they can borrow my mower. I can take out their bins.'

I suddenly think about my downstairs neighbour. I'm not getting on so well with her at the moment. I don't tell Hilton that. I just make a mental note: *Re-examine relationship with neighbour.*

'It's about how you treat people. That's the thing,' he says, like he's reading my thoughts again. 'We've only got two ways of communicating in this whole world, from the moment we leave our bedrooms in the morning till when we go back at night—words and actions are all you have. If your words and actions are beautiful, then your life is going to be beautiful, and you're going to make a difference in somebody's life. My prayer is that I help people. You gotta have an eye for need. You gotta be intentional. You gotta be intentional about your life, about how you live, you know? You don't need a university degree to figure out that if an old person is carrying a heavy load, you need to help him or her. You can see when someone is hitting the threshold of their capacity to do whatever it is they gotta do. So help them. It's in *doing* that you help someone. It may be a little thing. Insignificant. But at least its helping someone.'

I'm listening. He's helping me understand my own story a bit. Starting OzHarvest wasn't an accident. It was intentional, but in a way that I did not understand at the time. I knew I really wanted to know what it would feel like to live a life beyond surviving, making money and looking for pleasure. That was the deepest desire of my heart. And that led me to fix a problem that was right in front of me. But the ripple effect of fixing that problem was completely unknown to me. The effect on the food recipients, on the shelters, on the lives of my staff, on the community, on sustainability and climate change discourse—even the possibility of meeting a person like Hilton—is part of that ripple effect. My previously insular life would never have included that. I could never have imagined the richness that comes from having an eye for need.

'So that's purpose,' I say. 'To have an eye for need? To be kind . . .?'

He says, 'Purpose to me means meeting a need. Any sort of need. When I work out the front of my house, I talk to anything that moves. I don't have many gifts in life, but one gift I do have is that I can connect with just about any person on the street. That's how I do my work. One day I saw a fella walking up the footpath here, on a rainy day, with three kids under an umbrella. I yelled out, "Matey, why are you walking those kids to school out in the rain for? Can I give you a lift?"

'He said, "Oh, I have a car, but my battery is done."

'I said, "Hop into my car and we'll get your car going." From here to there he tells me he's out of work, his wife is out of work, and they pay $550 a week for rent, with three kids. So I jump-started the car. It began because I saw him walking his kids in the rain. You could say, "Oh, there's a fella going to school with his children, under an umbrella." And you could do nothing. But if we're going to have purpose, then obviously, you have to look out for a need. He's walking his kids to school in the rain!'

I'm floored, as usual, by the simple way he articulates things that I know, deep down, yet have never known how to say. In my work, it's become almost hard to use the word 'purpose', yet it seems that purpose is what so many people want. And they want me to help them find it. They want something to hold onto, to make them happy, fulfilled and found, yet what they also seek from purpose is to be seen and recognised for having found it. But the missing piece is that purpose is an inner understanding. It's an evolving place within each one of us that will bring meaning to absolutely anything any one of us puts our hand to. Purpose is about being alive in the best way we can. In Hilton's mode of living, purpose is a verb; it is in everything he does. There is no magic formula for finding purpose. But for those of us who are looking for a way to begin, maybe it starts with waking up and deciding to have an eye for need. Maybe it starts with that simple intention: today my purpose will be to notice ways that I could be kind, ways that I can look beyond what I normally see.

'Transformation is an individual thing,' he continues. 'We should show good precepts and good concepts right from the ground in our society. Every layer of your life is another floor of a building going up. Make it a stable building. Make it a beautiful building. So many people want to help people after they have been shown help and love. A few people I have helped now do what they saw me doing. They wanted to take things to the next level. I just got a text from a fella who went through our Salvos rehab back in 1989. He took over from me when I left to work with the homeless. And he sent me this text saying, "Hilton, this is what I have done this week." And I wrote back and said, "Mate, I'm so proud of what you do." A sentence of six or seven words. That's all I had to do. "I'm so proud of what you do." You can only do what you can do. But you gotta have an eye for it. Have an eye to see the need, to have the compassion. The ethos of love, the ethos of seeing past just what you see, and knowing what the people might need. That's kindness.'

Something about his line of thinking takes my mind to our free supermarket, and how afraid everyone was that people would take advantage of us. It was the first and most fervent question on everyone's lips. I suppose we've all helped someone and been taken advantage of. I suppose we've all learnt our lessons about that, and learnt to protect ourselves. 'Do you get taken advantage of Hilton? For your kindness?'

'Ah, I get taken for a ride all the time, Ronni. All the time. And I know I'm getting taken for a ride. You gotta be prepared for people taking advantage of you. But you gotta roll with some greedy in order to help the needy. Otherwise you start making judgements about that one greedy person. You can't make a judgement based on that one or a few experiences. Empathic compassion can't have judgement in it. You can't really tell people they can't have something. If they're greedy enough to take it, let them take it. I'll learn from that and take some simple measures next time to stop the same thing happening. I'll make sure other people get it first next time or something like that. There can be six bottles of two-litre milk over there and someone will grab the whole lot, with not a thought of the next fella. I say to them, "Be kind to one another." I always say that. Some people don't know that. They need to be gently shown appreciation and respect. Some people say they can pick who's needy and who's greedy. But I can't pick it. I've been around the traps for 57 years now, and I can't pick a greedy person from a needy person. You can't take it personally.'

He finishes off some chocolate cake. There is quiet for a moment. He remembers something that feels heavy somehow. 'There was this one day when I was a young officer in Mount Isa. I was in bed one time, and about half past two in the morning, this swaggie sort of fella bashes on my door. He needed something. Well, I went out and boy, did I give it to him. I said, "Listen, mate, what do you think you're doing, coming here, we got kids sleeping in the house," and la-de-da, but you know, God spoke to me then, inside my heart. This is what he said to me in my mind: "This man could have got that from anybody in this town. He didn't have to come here to hear that. He came to you. To hear something different."' Hilton can't go on now, he's crying, and through sobs says very quietly, 'But I took that correction. That was a lesson to me. I wish I had never said that. I sent him away sad. But that was a learning curve for me. To talk to people right. Real kindness. That's living faith.'

I've not heard the term 'living faith' before. Maybe it's a Christian term, so I ask him what it is. 'If we went down to Circular Quay right now, there may be a beautiful ocean liner there in the water. We'd say, "What a beautiful ocean liner." What we wouldn't see is the rudder. The rudder is in the water. In tonnage, it's only a small part of the boat really. But without that rudder, that ship couldn't go anywhere. To me, living faith is the rudder within your heart that guides you into good ways of living. If the rudder is in the right place, things don't go so askew. I am a red-blooded male. I've been tempted to do dumb stuff too. It's heartbreaking what happens when you get offcourse. You gotta set your sail right and it has to be in every element of your life. How you respond to people, how you talk to people. There are a lot of things I don't understand about God, I can tell you. There's a lot of questions I'll be asking when my time comes! But that's what I mean by a living faith.'

He continues. 'I'd rather have fish and chips on a river bank with a drunk than be around fancy people, you know? I'd rather knock around with a good old battler. I'd rather light a cigarette for someone, which I've done many times. That's the kind of love of Jesus. I wanna portray that sort of love. I want to serve people, without leading with a religious front. But rather with a practical approach to the given need that confronts me at the time. I may seem to be a bit irreverent sometimes, Ronni. But when you do four years in welfare and ten years in drug and alcohol and nine and a half years with prisoners, you lose your religious side. You don't lose your spirituality, but you stop that religious garbage that goes on. You can't maintain a one-eyed view of things in our line of work. I've lived in the real world where people have given me my pedigree in very unflattering terms. And you just roll with the punches. I've seen people come unstuck in life. Fellas that haven't got anything left. They've ruined their home. Their wives and children are gone. Their jobs are gone. They have criminal records. But worst of all, their self-esteem is gone. Everything is gone. I used to try and be a human jumper lead and come up beside them and put a bit of my faith into them and tell them that they can be better. They can.'

I can't imagine how you could really help someone in that kind of crisis. Like, really help them. 'How do you help that man, Hilton? How do we really help anyone, be it the unstuck woman or man or the many corrupt leaders in our society?'

He doesn't think for long. 'It became apparent to me throughout my life that it doesn't really matter what anyone believes, as long as they change in some way,' he says. 'I don't know how many times I went into the gaols and looked through that little hole in the prison cells and used to talk to those blokes. I used to go in that cell and say, "Come over, come over here, mate. Listen, it doesn't matter what you have done. You're a good person who has made a mistake. Just remember that. I can help you as much as you want me to help you. In the end, you have to do this work. Please don't be down on yourself. You're in here because you did the wrong thing. You can make a different choice." All of us can. It's so simple really. It's what Jesus taught.'

I like this Jesus stuff. Maybe my parents are rolling in their graves, but it's having a calming effect on me. Everything is so still in Hilton's garden all of a sudden. I think about Amma, my teacher in India. It's the same message. Doing good. Kindness. Serving something. Hinduism, Christianity, Buddhism, Islam— suddenly I can see all the little creeks running into the one river. 'I'm a strange sort of a Christian really,' Hilton says. 'I don't really care whether Noah put all the animals in the ark. I couldn't give a stuff. Or whether Jonah was really swallowed by the whale. All I care about is that when I get up in the morning I'm a decent guy until I go to bed at night. That's all I really care about. It frustrates the hell out of some people, because I don't care. There's nothing else in life to me apart from being a good person. And trying to share that goodness with other people.'

'And yet there's so much emphasis on gaining and protecting material things . . .' I say.

'There's nothing wrong with being rich, Ronni. But if someone's richness doesn't reach out, it's a shame. Despite this, the milk of human kindness never goes dry. People are so kind. Many people like helping their fellow man. So many people volunteer. So many people. The milk of human kindness never goes dry.'

I'm crying again. Sixteen years down this road and it's true. The milk of human kindness has never run dry. I can attest to that. From the volunteers to the donors, from my staff to our corporate partners, to all these incredible people I meet every day. No matter the challenges and uncertainties going on in our world, there is so much human kindness happening too, and that is what is going to see us all through. We just need to open our eyes to it. 'Life is incredible,' I say, 'that it's brought us to this moment together. I'm so lucky to have met you.'

'I could never have dreamed I'd have the life I'd have,' my friend says. 'Me. A nobody from Gympie. God makes something of nothing. So much can be made out of not much.'

I don't know that much about Christianity, but I know I have never heard the Christian message quite like this. It's a human message. There's poetry in it. I can't stop thinking about my book now. Hilton will be in it. This conversation. His work and his simple genius. 'Hilton, what would you tell an audience of people if you had a chance to share your most important words with them?' He doesn't hesitate for a second. He says, 'Don't think about yourself too much. Think about others. And in thinking about others, suddenly, you'll become incredibly happy. Think about someone in your life who needs a bit of help. Start with that. Go help them. We can all share that. It starts off at home and then it will emanate everywhere.'

I suddenly feel that time is closing in on us and that I'm holding him up. He's got to go pick up a truck for someone, help them move, take them some furniture. I look at my phone. I'm late to my next meeting. We stand up, shake off crumbs and scrunched-up tissues. We hug. I don't want to let go. But I have to. 'One little starfish at a time . . .' he says under his breath, as he hugs me and then lets go. And with that, I walk out into the blazing sun, back into the world, his sublime garden still very much alive on my sweltering skin.

# CHAPTER 39

# THE RIPPLE EFFECT

What has happened over the years with OzHarvest, my little side project baby, staggers me, and it just keeps growing. We rescue food all across Australia. We currently have 220 staff members nationally, of which 120 are drivers, and a fleet of more than 60 vehicles. It takes twenty million dollars a year to run this national organisation and we are funded completely philanthropically. That's a hell of a lot of very generous people and an enormous amount of fundraising! We rescue almost two hundred tonnes of beautiful quality food a week and deliver it to more than 1300 different charities. We run many different educational programs, such as NEST (Nutrition Education Sustenance Training), Nourish, FEAST (Food Education and Sustainability Training) and Cooking for a Cause to ensure that we teach how to minimise food waste and create changemakers in our community. We've published two OzHarvest cookbooks, with 50 of Australia's finest chefs giving their best and favourite recipes using leftovers, as well as a children's book about sustainability, called *Lenny and the Ants*, written by Jessica Chapnik Kahn and illustrated by Matthew Martin.

We run campaigns on food waste, and our lobbying led Australia to commit to halving food waste by 2030, in alignment with the United Nations Sustainable Development Goals.

Our statistics show that every three seconds a meal is being delivered through OzHarvest. I'm so proud of that. Even when I'm sitting at home feeling content or tired or with my family, I know that our work just keeps on happening. Sometimes I just sit quietly and say to myself, *It's there.* The very core of our purpose—to nourish our country—is taking place. It blows my mind.

Our upcoming project is Refettorio OzHarvest Sydney, which is a collaboration with 'Food for Soul', the organisation conceived by Italian chef Massimo Bottura. 'Refettorio' comes from the Latin *reficere*, meaning to restore or to remake, because this is a place designed to restore faith, and to inspire and empower human potential. It will be no ordinary restaurant! This restaurant will bring together those in greatest need and those who have enough to give. The community kitchen will serve free lunches made from rescued food for those who need it, and at night it will be a fully functioning restaurant, open to the public. Night times will fund the daytime social kitchen. Fabulous chefs will each donate one night a year, so you will never know which five-star chef may be cooking for you. This beautiful project will be housed in our three-storey sustainable terrace house, bought for this very purpose by the Matana Foundation. It will be filled with art and music. It's the perfect way to combine food and hospitality with art and culture!

And that's just in Australia. In 2014, we partnered with the UN to activate global events around zero waste. We've also helped to train people in Peru, Italy, Spain, Thailand and many other countries, to use our model of sustainability within their own cities and their own culture. We share our model and brand, very different from the Angel Harvest model originally shared with me, to create and support UKHarvest, under the patronage of the Duchess of Cornwall, and KiwiHarvest in New Zealand. Both these were possible thanks to investment from our friends at the Goodman Foundation, who continue to share their love.

Finally, in 2017, after years of plotting and planning, and to my immense joy, South Africa Harvest was born. I cannot tell you how important and how poignant this was for me. I gave Israel my youth. I gave Australia my talents and OzHarvest. But I felt as though I had not given South Africa any part of myself. I'd wished for so long that I had contributed in some way. But I hadn't. For this reason, from a personal perspective, SAHarvest is something very beautiful and very meaningful that has happened in my lifetime. Nineteen million people in South Africa experience food vulnerability each day. The food is there, it just needs rescuing, and we are doing our part to make that happen. And you know what is even more amazing? Alan Browde, my childhood husband-to-be, is the CEO of SAHarvest! We had stayed connected throughout our whole lives, and Alan had watched OzHarvest flourish in Australia. He had been on his own quest throughout the years to find meaningful work. The timing was impeccable.

A few times a year I schedule in my diary a day of driving in an OzHarvest van with one of our 40 drivers. The routes are too sophisticated now for me to do on my own, as I did in the old days. It's a tight operation and the most efficient pick-up routes have been organised so carefully it's become a fine art. It's a delight to watch our drivers do it so skilfully. The reason it's a priority for me to go out in the van and rescue food is that it's important for me to reconnect with where this all began. I'm not at the coalface anymore. I don't get the full satisfaction of physically dropping off food, like I used to. My days are full of future planning, meetings, strategising, innovation, fundraising, travelling, keynote speaking, mentoring, paperwork, and millions of emails. It's every aspect of managing a business. And some tasks are more enjoyable than others.

It would be very easy to get lost in the bits and pieces that go into keeping something running. It would be very easy to start living only for the bits that are enjoyable, and not so much for the others. And often people ask me how I keep the passion alive. 'What's the secret? What keeps you energised?' Let me share with you what inspires me daily.

A few years ago, I was invited to talk to 5000 fifteen-year-olds at the Sydney Convention Centre. My talk came straight after artist, comedian, actor and author Anh Do, who was too divine for words. He was funny, popular, inspiring and he looks like he's fifteen himself. It was a hard act to follow. Here I was, middle-aged and likely to be bloody boring to them. I was quite daunted thinking about how I would engage so many teenagers. But I was determined to have some fun. I got up there and launched into the story of OzHarvest, and I must have somehow rocked it, because I could feel they were present and engaged. There was silence. That's always the best sign. At the end of my talk, there was a Q&A, and from the very back row came my first question. A kid in a hoodie shuffled to the microphone. I couldn't see his face. And he said, 'Firstly, I want to thank you because I've been a recipient of OzHarvest food, and it helped me enormously. Secondly, can you tell me what happens to you when you've had a bad day?'

I'm always taken aback when I talk to young people, because they ask me the most profound questions. 'Thank you for the courage of sharing that OzHarvest has provided food for you. I feel so happy to know we could help,' I said, with a lump in my throat, because admitting in front of so many of his peers that he had needed food from us was a very courageous thing to do. I was also so moved that we'd helped this young man. 'As far as your question about what happens to me when I've had a bad day. Firstly, I make it a practice to always wake up with gratitude for the day ahead. I've chosen to live a life that consciously chooses the kind of day I want to have, and the only person who can choose that for me is me. If I slip into a bad day, I remind myself that's a choice. And if I'm satisfied with that choice, I allow myself that bad day. But after examining how I got there, I will always try and reach for a better thought. And I try to bring the awareness that no one is responsible for that bad day. Many aspects of that bad day are in my hands—my reaction, my thoughts around it, how I talk to myself. My thoughts are *my* choice. And I always like to choose thoughts in the realm of gratitude. I will always choose gratitude wherever I can, from the minute I open my eyes, and especially so on a bad day.'

He took a moment and then said, 'I think you may have just changed my life forever. And I have one more question. Could I please have a hug?' I cried out, 'Absolutely!' He bounded down like a puppy towards the stage and I jumped down. Can you imagine the boldness of this boy, his emotional intelligence? By this stage, I was bawling big time. I still couldn't see his face. But we hugged for what seemed like ages. I was so overwhelmed that when someone yelled out, 'How do we get a hold of you?' I actually gave out my personal email to 5000 kids. I consequently received about 300 emails, many of them saying, 'I wish I'd been able to get a hug.'

A month later, I was giving a talk to a bunch of university students and I looked to the corner and saw a boy in a hoodie. I just knew it was him. When I finished my talk, he came over to me and introduced himself. His name was Paniora Nukunuku. It turns out he was travelling from far away to come to a lot of my talks. We exchanged details. From that day on, Pani and I became friends. I check in with him from time to time, and he knows he can always contact me. The whole OzHarvest family is here for him, he knows that. Since we met, he's volunteered at OzHarvest now and then. He won an Amplifier Award after he got involved in the Canterbury Youth Council, then went on to win the Youth Volunteer of the Year award from the Foundation for Young Australians. He has now completed his studies in youth work and is a youth worker for local government, to help other young people who face homelessness and mental health issues.

Stories like this happen to me on a weekly basis. What OzHarvest does has such an impact that there isn't much I have to do to feel inspired. I just turn up and these stories unfold. I am now the lucky beneficiary of what OzHarvest does. These stories are so 'real'. I have enough 'real' that connects me with what I'm doing in my everyday life to energise all the rest. OzHarvest started by being about filling stomachs. But this story is the evolution of that, it's about what food enables a person to become. Food gave Pani the sustenance and nourishment to go out into the world and show up. It's a ripple effect of 'bigger'. Today, I received an email from someone saying, 'I just want you to know that I've organised an event at a hotel, and I've arranged for OzHarvest to pick up the leftover food.' That means so much to me. Because every day someone is able to make this kind of choice based on the fact that we are operating.

The other day I was crossing the street in my OzHarvest T-shirt and people started calling out 'We love OzHarvest!' I am stopped on the street by strangers who tell me they just want to hug me, or that they have been impacted by OzHarvest. A woman stopped me recently on the street and said, 'Thank you.'

'I'm not sure why you are thanking me,' I said.

'My child was completely uncontrollable at school,' she said. 'We had no food, he couldn't concentrate. We started getting food from OzHarvest. And he got through school. He's now at university. I thank you and bless you every day.' I mean, what do you say? How do I get my head around that? It's a very real and quantifiable differ-ence that is happening every day. And this energises me. Every driver has a story to share with me. Every person delivering food has a story to tell me. Every volunteer has a story too. And every one of those stories is a very big deal to me. It's beyond me that a simple fix to my personal food-waste issue became someone's university degree. How could I not feel the daily thrill of these privileges?

Just thinking about our Nourish kids' program literally gets me up every morning. Nourish takes vulnerable kids between the ages of fifteen and 25, and puts them through a six-month life skills and hospitality training program that is fundamentally transformative. It's transformative because these kids have never had a successful learning experience. They've either been kicked out of school or they've dropped out of school. They've had no role model for what success looks like. These kids walk in our doors looking down at the floor. They often have no ability to make eye contact. They leave six months later telling us we opened a door within them that they didn't even know existed. These are kids whose social skills were limited. They are now standing, proud and tall, at their own graduation ceremony, holding the first physical embodiment of their success: their graduation certificate.

These young people give us their precious trust. And then, when they graduate, I feel privileged to meet their parents (or their foster carers or their social workers), who inevitably take my hands in theirs, look me in the eyes with tears and say, 'OzHarvest changed not just my boy's life but my family's life. He couldn't keep down a job, he wouldn't show up to work. But here he is, graduating.' That boy came into our kitchen, found a vocation and found something meaningful. He learnt how to earn a living and look after himself. It gave him confidence, and a newfound ability to make choices about the kind of life he wanted to live.

So yes, the hard bits that sometimes come up when managing a business can feel debilitating, but not debilitating enough to make a dent, to spoil my day. Not ever. The love that's coming back at me is too great. The challenges, however, I never brush off. I use them to examine myself, to ask, *Am I still the right person to be running this organisation? Could someone else do it better?* I assess now in a way I never have before. I think it's absolutely what I should be doing, after sixteen years. And I am committed to being as effective as I can be.

The things that unfold from fixing a problem, following an urge or a passion project—we can never know where they will lead, how they will affect the world. These outcomes are not within our control, they are beyond us. Our job is simply to follow the call, follow the crumbs.

CHAPTER 40

# SPIRITUAL SUSTAINABILITY

For the past sixteen years I have been called a disrupter, and there is definitely some truth to that. There is no doubt that OzHarvest has disrupted the food supply chain. No one was reusing surplus fresh produce when I started, because the norm in Australia was that excess food was thrown away. OzHarvest fundamentally changed the way this country looked at leftovers and, in turn, the notion that it is unconscionable for good food to go to waste. But it's a funny thing. Because in fact, when you think about it, the real disruption is the food waste, not me. The real disruption is what has stood in the way of our planet's natural state of being. Food waste is not natural. The animal and plant kingdoms know that. All living organisms in nature are inherently resourceful. They know how to sustain themselves. Wasting and neglecting precious resources is not natural. It's not a part of the fabric of our ecosystem. It is our connection to nature and the ability to work with it, not against it, that creates harmony and balance to serve our planet best.

Awareness of not wasting food, recycling, composting, reducing our consumption, caring about climate change, minimising landfill and pollution, eliminating fossil fuels and reducing the use of plastics is growing daily, but it's still not at a pace that is sustainable for our planet. Our choices and behaviour about sustainability have been made easier, as there is much more overt knowledge available, and it's an important move in the right direction. But often, I will still hear from friends, even my most environmentally active friends, that deep down they feel despondency creeping in. They express to me that the sustainable decisions they make in their household, in a world of billions, does not feel significant enough to repair the problems we are creating for our planet. Where things may be headed scares them. And, I must admit, I understand these feelings well. Every day it can feel like we do more, and yet no matter how many documentaries we watch or produce, and no matter how many memes we read or create, and no matter how many petitions we sign or rallies we attend, the way the wider world is computing the message doesn't feel like it's moving fast enough. It feels as though unless every single one of us on the planet participates in sustainable choices, we cannot fully do the job of restoration and repair. Although our efforts are supremely worthwhile, the rate of change feels too slow for what science is telling us we need to achieve.

Many of us have put a lot of energy into changing our behaviour. We advocate the use of BYO shopping bags, reusable cups and metal straws, composting, repurposing clothes, going plastic-free. Every one of these efforts is hugely valuable, especially en masse!

There is science to prove that they are having a positive effect on our planet. We must continue. But I think there is more to this than sustainable behaviour. We need a deeper change. Some days, from where I'm standing, sharing the message of how we need to change our behaviour feels like trying to get people to do a bunch of homework: 'Do it because it's the right thing to do.' It feels like just another subject at school, yet another something we have to do and 'get through'. There seems to be a missing vital and engaging piece in the puzzle about environmental change.

Now, I risk sounding didactic, but I feel this message is important enough to take that risk. There is a crucial element that's missing in the sustainability discourse, and it's this: the sustainability of our planet is dependent on the way we treat one another and the way we treat ourselves. In other words, how we treat one another and ourselves goes hand in hand with the future of our planet. There is no one in the world who is not participating in this exchange. The only question is how we are each contributing. If we are causing some degree of harm to those around us or even to ourselves, how does this reflect on the world around us?

Dealing with food waste has taught me that there is no battle, no campaign and no cause that can be won without combatting the ignorance that lies within ourselves. When I transform myself, I don't just transform myself: I transform the world around me. This may sound simplistic. This may sound trite. But there is more to this than meets the eye. When we truly consider this kind of inner work, when we analyse how we treat the people around us, how we treat ourselves; when we become aware of the harm we cause, we begin the process of no longer serving just our own individuality.

We become a part of one another; we take care of one another. We can no longer turn our backs on suffering. We no longer want to repeat the mistakes of the past. We will find we are suddenly asking ourselves questions such as, *What does the world most need from me at this time? What is working? What do I want the future to look like for my children and other people's children?* All of these questions mean we are well on our way to truly taking care of our planet. Doing this work means naturally considering the earth. The planet becomes a part of us; we each become the planet. We are not just 'doing' or 'having to do'. We are experiencing our world and our connectedness through the way we live.

Wanting to take part in the work of inner transformation requires deep reflection on our inner lives and facing our shortcomings bravely. It means looking at our everyday actions, our relationships with the people around us, where we blame, how we complain, where we discriminate, where we feel resentment, where we are self-destructive and how we hurt others. This awareness will bring clues as to how our inner world is affecting our outer world. It is a step forward in wholeness for ourselves and our planet. It is a yes to living lives steeped in goodness.

If we want to talk about disruption, this is the great disruption. The great disruption is letting go of doing and hoping and blaming and fearing, and starting to be the change you want to see in the world, to paraphrase Gandhi. Connecting with ourselves and each other is an important way we can bring peace to our planet. It will inherently help us—stop us from misusing our precious energy, day in and day out, in jobs we hate, in cycles of survival and money and despair and depression. We are hurting each other. We are hurting ourselves. It is no wonder we are hurting the planet. We forget to consider that every second of every day there are ways of serving each other. Of bringing value. Of going full out at whatever we do and treating people—all people, even strangers—with kindness.

We each have a different story. Some of us are happy but want to make a difference. Some of us believe it's too late to do what we love. Some of us are fulfilled now and then. Some of us are confused as to what we want to pursue. There are a million scenarios. Irrespective of where you are at in your life—what you know or don't know— how you live matters. When we relate to ourselves and one another with kindness, with authenticity and with dignity, we will in turn positively impact our environment. We will care in a different way. Take a moment to consider how you treat the people in your life. Our relationship with others reflects something about our relation- ship with the planet. They go hand in hand. Please let's not forget that. Please let's realise our potential. And please let's keep using our BYO shopping bags.

# CHAPTER 41

# ONE WARM EGG

One of my team shared this beautiful piece of Aboriginal wisdom with me. Never take all the eggs from a nest. Always leave one egg for the future. Take three eggs for yourself, not four. Allow the possibility of procreation, of multiplication. If you take all the eggs, how can anything else be born?

Well, doesn't this idea make so much sense? It seems fundamental. We've been taking everything there is from Mother Nature's nest for so long that we barely even notice we are doing it. Whether we like it or not, leaving the nest empty is robbing and pillaging the planet, and limiting our potential. The simple wisdom of leaving an egg ensures the sustainability of our future. Wouldn't embracing this Indigenous wisdom be a noble legacy for us to leave behind, as visitors on Planet Earth?

When I speak about legacy in my talks, or when I am mentoring, people seem really interested and want to discover what it might mean for them. I think people generally associate legacy with something that requires a grand scale, recognition and big works, something that involves having a lot of money. I fundamentally do *not* believe legacy is just for rich people. I believe it is for everyone. Legacy is a vital piece of the future that involves all of us. Sustainability and living an aligned and valuable life are not just for the wealthy. It certainly does help to have money, in order to make choices or to leave behind wonderful things like scholarships and bequests when we die, but to me, this is not and never will be where legacy begins and ends.

From my perspective, legacy involves a contribution to the world, one that is beyond just ourselves. It has everything to do with the purpose of being born human. I began thinking about legacy on the day I started dropping food at random shelters, because that is the day I started feeding ten people. Before then I hadn't fed any apart from my own family. And then those ten people became a hundred. And then a hundred became a thousand, and a thousand became ten thousand. It escalated, but that is not necessarily the point. The point is that one small action was put into motion in the world that hadn't existed before, that helped someone. That small thing could multiply, did multiply and will multiply, even when I am well and truly gone.

I believe that the spark of every human who has ever lived means something. It's not nothing. If we forget that spark, it's lost, but it doesn't have to be lost. Research shows that people wonder on their deathbeds if and how they will be remembered—those who have the opportunity to contemplate this before dying, that is. It is only then that many consider what they are leaving behind. Often there is regret for what they never did or said. The idea of our bodies and our possessions disappearing into nothingness is one that is hard to get our heads around. No one really wants to think about it. But whether we think about it or not, it appears we are born with a sense of wanting to leave something behind. This desire seems to live in the inner recesses of each human being. We seek to bring light into our world; we want to bring value and goodness. It is a wisdom that is innate, residing in all of us. To me, it's important to talk to our donors about their legacy, because that is what donation is really about—enabling long-lasting impact on the world around us. I talk to volunteers about legacy, because that is what giving your time is all about. I talk to young people about legacy, because the younger we start, the more we can do with the time we have on earth.

Many years ago, I received a phone call out of the blue from a guy who said, 'I'd love to volunteer for OzHarvest one day a week.' I said, 'Come on in! Let's talk.' In those days, I personally met every single volunteer who wanted to work with us. Kev Wallace came in and he was delightful. He had great skills. He had just retired and sold his business, and was wanting to give back. It turns out he'd offered his services to many charities, but they'd knocked him back because they couldn't see his value. What a loss for them! He was brilliant. By the end of the interview, we were chatting like old friends. He was the kind of guy who you instantly felt you'd known for a very long time. I accompanied him to his car and lo and behold, he was completely on brand. He opened the door to a yellow-and-black Mustang. I said, 'Kev, you're obviously made for us.' I knew there and then that it was a match made in heaven.

Within a very short period, Kev was working for us three days a week, running the logistics of all our casual drivers. It was a big job, and his project management skills were fantastic. He loved working for OzHarvest and told me he'd never been happier in all his working life. He used to wear a yellow OzHarvest T-shirt every time he went on holidays. He'd travel to far-flung, obscure places and he'd send me photos of himself wearing that T-shirt from all these locations around the world. He told me he did it so the fairy dust of OzHarvest could be sprinkled all over the globe.

One day, Kev called and said, 'Ronni, I'm not coming in today. I have to go to the hospital. I'm not well. I've been diagnosed with lung cancer and I don't know how long I have to live.'

Swallowing the lump in my throat and feigning strength I said, 'Kev, take your laptop to hospital, because don't think for a second that we can live without you. We're not letting you go so easily!' But he never came back to work with us again.

It had been weeks since we'd seen Kev, and then one day his partner Chris called to let us know that she was bringing him in; he wanted to come in for a visit, one last time. I guess it was his farewell. He was so frail, it was terribly hard to see him like that. All the staff came down to greet him. We all loved him very much. Chris had brought him specifically to see our new yellow vans that had just come in. Kev loved cars. That was one of his passions. He was thrilled to see the new branding. He thought it was so snazzy. But most of all he loved the new bright and shiny yellow-and-black vans. And while we were standing there, admiring the vehicles, he glanced in the direction of my ten-year-old red Prius, parked next to one of the vans. Kev looked at my car and suddenly turned to me and said, 'Ronni, I want you to go and buy yourself a brand-new yellow Prius. OzHarvest yellow. Everyone should see the CEO of OzHarvest when she's on the road, sprinkling her fairy dust.'

'Kev, that's mad,' I said. 'Why don't we just paint my red Prius yellow?'

'No way,' he replied. 'I need you to take this gift from me. I want you to have a new yellow car. I want that yellow fairy dust to be sprinkled.' I looked at him and just bowed my head. I could feel this meant a lot to him. I had to graciously accept.

In the loving care of his partner Chris, our beautiful Kev died a few weeks later. We were all still walking around the office with heavy hearts when, as synchronicity would have it, one day before his wake, his yellow Prius gift arrived. It was a sight to behold. I'd had the car branded on the bonnet with a big black heart, emblazoned with our purpose: 'Nourishing Our Country'. Each side door bore the words 'OzHarvest loves Kev and Chris'. He would have loved that car. In that moment, I desperately wished he could have seen it.

I was invited to the wake and I asked if I could say a few words to honour Kev. I drove up in my new car and they had left a space for me to park, right in front of the entrance to the hall. You could not miss this car. The pallbearers walked right past it with his coffin, and I believe Kev got to see it, and read the words 'OzHarvest Loves Kev and Chris'. And so did everybody else who was there. In that very moment it was clear to me that *he* was the fairy dust, sprinkled everywhere he went.

The hall was jam-packed with people who shared stories of Kev's generosity, kindness and thoughtfulness; he was known for these qualities by everyone. I was privileged to share the profound contribution he made to the world through OzHarvest. I also found out through the speeches that when Kev went out with one of our drivers to deliver food, if he noticed something that could be useful to someone at a shelter—a TV, a kettle, a radio—he would take it upon himself to make sure it magically appeared at the shelter, anonymously, the next day. He gave for the sake of giving. That was Kev.

To this day, at least a couple of times a week, on seeing my car, someone will ask me, 'Why does OzHarvest love Kev and Chris?' And I have the opportunity to talk about him. I talk about how he helped us create the logistics for our drivers, how his generosity meant we were able to offer more food to people, more efficiently. There are people right now in Sydney who can be reached and fed because of our Kev. Every time I talk about him, I believe I extend his life. Blessed be his memory, his kindness and his love.

Each person has a different situation. I don't know if you are rich or poor, old or young. I don't know where you live and I don't know who you know or what you care about. None of that matters, however, when it comes to legacy. What I would like to do is urge you to think about it. Will your legacy live on in your children, in the values you have taught them? Will it live on through the environmental program you urged your kids' school to adopt? Through the togetherness you brought to your apartment block, or the students you encouraged to believe in themselves, or the value you brought to your office, or the time you put into helping people? Each and every one of us not only has opportunities, but has the full capacity and capability to be a change-maker. Governments and leaders may let us down. But as an individual you have the power to shift things for the good. Don't let anything stop you. Your light is tenacious. And when you realise that you have those bright little seeds inside of you, you will start asking yourself the right questions. What can I give? What can I leave behind? Am I leaving one warm egg in the nest? Whoever you are, wherever you are, your legacy will live on.

# CHAPTER 42

# CHOCOLATE CAKE

It's Saturday morning and I feel like baking a cake for my little grandson, Lev. Chocolate cake is his favourite and, let's face it, my favourite too; it's a twofold treat. I look in the pantry—I don't have flour. Maybe I can grind up some almonds to make almond flour. I don't have vanilla essence either, but I do have cloves. So I'll improvise. I'm going out on a limb here and who knows what's about to happen. Maybe I should pull out a recipe? Who am I kidding, I'm not very good at following recipes. I'm going to give this a go. Generally, it works out fine, and sometimes it works out even better.

I'm stirring and I'm slicing and I'm grating and I'm sifting, while I think about chocolate cake and the unexpected honour of writing this book. Writing it has connected so many dots for me. Telling my story in public has glossed over so much—there is a limit to what you can say in a 30-minute keynote! But sitting down, digging deep and putting pen to paper has shown me what each person, place, experience—both wanted and unwanted—has given me. The countries I've lived in have each imbued me with qualities that were elemental to those places at those times. South Africa showed me injustice, so I could work to create justice within myself. Israel showed me equality and war, so that I could work to create peace and harmony within myself. Australia showed me opportunity, so that I could work with my hands, my voice, my imagination, my abilities. My con-man lover brought me to simplicity and humility. Living on my own for the last years of my life has shown me what true independence means, how aloneness reveals your inner power, how family and friends are precious jewels. Perhaps the limitations within our societies are gifts life offers us to make our world better. We grow, we learn, we find our purpose.

This new and unexpected OzHarvest journey that began in middle age has shown me that purpose is a way of living your life. It's a life lived more simply. It always starts in the moment. It's an inner experience of deciding to live each moment in a way that brings value to yourself and others, in a way that is important to you. Some people call it meaning, some call it dharma, some call it sacred work, some call it 'your calling'. For me, the minute you start doing anything in your life with the intention of noticing people—especially those right in front of you—and of applying the principles of kindness, gratitude and generosity, that's when all these things fall into place. That is the stuff of bliss.

Repurposing my life turned everything around and added a dimension I didn't know existed. I didn't even know it was happening until it happened. OzHarvest remade me. I was looking for something, but had no sense that this would in fact be the redesigning of me. I didn't do it consciously in that sense. I never said to myself, I'm going to go out there and start a charity. I didn't worry about any of that. I didn't have to. Other forces take care of those things. It was simply aligning with something deep within myself. I never knew I could evolve into someone who could lead, manage, talk and inspire people, let alone change anything in the fabric of society. I am still in wonderment about all of that. I don't take it for granted for a single second. Even as I finish writing this book, there's a voice in my head that says, *Who are you to do and say any of these things?* But I know there is a truer voice that says, *Who are you not to do this?*

Life is rarely a tried and tested recipe. It takes courage to work with unknown ingredients—like a morning in Soweto, a failed relationship, an event with untouched food. In my case, that cooked up a life that enabled rescued food to turn into more than 150 million meals for those who need them. The unknown flavours us, changes us, makes use of our unique capabilities and ultimately helps us become the best we can be, if we allow it.

Creating a better world within and without is a work in progress. Sometimes it's hard. Sometimes it feels hopeless. Sometimes it's a big experiment. Sometimes it doesn't quite work out and it collapses and falls apart. My chocolate cake may do that. I'll know in 27 minutes! But I'm showing up, I'm participating. And if it doesn't work, I'll start again. Like I've started again so many times in my life. It doesn't have to be based on anything in the past. It can be something new, something different, something I haven't tasted before, something I could never have imagined.

The smell of chocolate cake always reminds me of my mother, and of my childhood days of baking, and icing and delivering all those hundreds of cakes. It is the smell of finding the possible in the impossible. It is the smell of resilience. It is the reward of licking a bowl of cake mix at the end of the day.

Lev bounds through the door, bringing me back to the present. 'Safi,' he says, 'Mama said you have chocolate cake for me?' I pull my improvised creation out of the oven. 'It's hot,' I warn. I look at his little face, his big blue eyes and that crease of expectation on his forehead. He is a dream to me. So fresh, so new, a vision of the world yet to come. 'I can't wait, Safi, I want it now,' he squeals. I hand him a warm slice of chocolate sponge. His face crinkles up in delight. 'Safi, this cake is different. I love it.'

# AFTERWORD

When I was seventeen years old, I found the Israeli writer Amos Oz. I had just landed in Israel and was learning to speak Hebrew, when my Hebrew teacher gave us the book, *My Michael*, to read. It was 1970, and although Oz had written only three books then, he was already becoming an icon. I read the book from cover to cover, to improve my Hebrew and to try to understand the culture behind the language in which it was written. I needed help with some words, and it was very hard, but I loved the exercise. I remember feeling proud that I'd managed to read one of his books in Hebrew. Despite the difficulty of the exercise, I could hear his gentle power, his poetic voice. It was his voice that in decades to follow would become a moral compass for the whole country—Jews and Palestinians alike—a voice of unwavering hope and belief that peace would reign, a voice that advocated conversation and communication between all people. And that voice, that man, never gave up, even in the face of disappointing injustices. Of the 40 books Amos Oz wrote in his lifetime, for some reason *My Michael* is the only one I've ever read.

Forty-nine years later, however, Amos Oz found me. I was invited to make a little speech about him at a tribute event, after he died in 2018. I was given a short piece of his writing to read out, and this is what it said:

> I believe that if one person is watching a huge calamity, let's say a conflagration, a fire, there are always three principle options:
>
> a. Run away, as far away and as fast as you can and let those who cannot run burn.
> b. Write a very angry letter to the editor of your paper demanding that the responsible people be removed from office with disgrace. Or, for that matter, launch a demonstration.
> c. Bring a bucket of water and throw it on the fire, and if you don't have a bucket, bring a glass, and if you don't have a glass, use a teaspoon, everyone has a teaspoon. And yes, I know a teaspoon is little and the fire is huge, but there are millions of us and each one of us has a teaspoon.
>
> Now I would like to establish the Order of the Teaspoon. People who share my attitude, not the run-away attitude or the letter attitude, but the teaspoon attitude—I would like them to walk around wearing a little teaspoon on the lapel of their jackets, so that we know that we are in the same movement, in the same brotherhood, in the same order, the Order of the Teaspoon.

The night I read this piece of writing, I could barely sleep. The excerpt was so powerful, so breathtaking to me, that I barely knew what to do with myself. I knew there had been times in my life when

I had run away from the fire, that's for sure. I also knew that creating OzHarvest had been one of my decisions not to run away from something challenging. But this teaspoon idea was way bigger than starting a charity or doing something that the world deemed 'big'. This teaspoon idea was very simple. It was an everyday thing. It was a wake-up-in-the-morning and be-the-person-you-want-to-be thing. Serve something. In my case: my children, my family, my friends, my neighbours, my staff, strangers; all of them. I tossed and turned in bed, amazed at how deeply Oz's words resonated. As someone involved with food, of course I loved the notion of the teaspoon. But the teaspoon as symbol of human capacity to do good took flight in my mind, in a way that I could barely contain. This was universal. His words sang and sang in my mind till morning. My teaspoon grew wings.

The very next day, without hesitation, I put a teaspoon in my pocket. I had a feeling it would come in handy, even though I wasn't sure how. As it turned out, on that particular day OzHarvest did a training session for executives from a major corporation, and I was brought in to do the finale. I decided to finish my talk with Oz's words, and at the end I pulled out my teaspoon and asked if anyone wanted to take it, and join the Order of the Teaspoon. Before I'd even finished the words, a guy leapt up and approached me, 'My name is Allan Mills and you have no idea how much I need this. This is my right time.' I could see in his eyes that he was experiencing something profound, just as I had when I had read the words for the first time. There was that deep, humbling resonance. I could see this little teaspoon was giving him permission to do or be something in the world in a way that he had always wanted to be. It was simple. That was the power of the teaspoon.

It wasn't long before I had to go to his company office for a meeting. I'd barely walked in when I was told that Allan wanted to see me first. Allan arrived with a big smile on his face, and a really big envelope that looked heavy. He handed it to me and said, 'I took my son on the weekend, and we went from thrift shop to thrift shop. We bought you these teaspoons so that you would have a lasting supply to give to people. I wanted others to experience the power of the teaspoon, just as I have.' Well, I just couldn't believe it. He had absolutely got it. His teaspoon had multiplied, and he had involved his son in that act of generosity! That is the full circle. His action had initiated him into the Order of the Teaspoon, and all it took was a decision.

From that day on, I started taking a teaspoon with me to every speaking gig I was doing. I have hugged grown executive men, and let them bawl in my arms. I have received bulk boxes and bags of teaspoons from people, who thought I might need them. And I have watched the power of a single person choosing to live from their heart in a single moment, to start doing what felt really valuable to them, to start living in the way they'd always wanted to. Because the truth is, dear reader, that that teaspoon is your birthright. You were born with it. Open your hands, take a look. Can you see it? Its silver, smooth edges are there for you, and have always been there for you. It lives in your heart. It is your heart. Now all you have to do is start using it.

# ACKNOWLEDGEMENTS

With huge gratitude to:

My wonderful, ever-present sisters, Pam and Margie—one set of parents, one childhood, but so many different memories.

Florrie—wherever she may be—for her indelible, unconditional love.

Paul Browde and Caroline Lambert for starting me on this journey of telling my story with encouragement, curiosity and insight.

Nathalie Latham for her divine wisdom in leading me to my perfect writing partner.

Romina Mandrini who read my words and gave me so much time, advice, feedback and the courage to continue.

My right-hand woman, Marla Minow, for thoughtfully and creatively carving out time for Jessy and I to write this book.

Colin Fainberg, Mark Barrett, Anthony Kahn, Julie White, Elaine Booth, Jane Matthews, Ilona Lee, Lesley Gild, Oscar Shub, Rob Tulloch, Rachel Argaman, Richard Deutsch and Lawrence Goldstone, who have been fundamental parts of repurposing my life.

Sri Sakthi Narayani Amma for being my guiding light.

Selma Browde, Hilton Harmer and Rob Kelly for sharing and inspiring me to be a better human being.

Alan Browde for a lifelong friendship that birthed the dream of South Africa Harvest.

Des Kahn and Irving Wallach for companionship, life-changing growth and love.

Michael Frankel for his legal expertise.

Dan Goldberg for his continual generosity and support.

Donna Sife for sharing her stories with me whenever I need them.

Michael Zhu for letting me call him at all hours and being the most caring and generous tech expert in the world.

Bauer Media for generously digging up files.

My publishing team at Murdoch Books: Jane Morrow and Lou Johnson for believing in the value of this story and all their amazing work; Julie Mazur Tribe and Alison Fraser for their greater vision and incredible talents of refinement; Trisha Garner and Susanne Geppert for their design work; and Carol Warwick for publicity.

My OzHarvest family—every one of you—for changing my life and inspiring me daily.

My besties (they know who they are) for supporting me through many long years of precious friendship.

Lev, Lalita and Rishi for making me a Safi, and Emily for the gifts of Beau and Jasmine.

My precious sons, Nadav and Edo, who encouraged these words to come forth and always give me so much faith in love and goodness.

Jessica Chapnik Kahn, my co-writer and friend/daughter/sister/parent from another life, for her love, patience, skill and wizardry in bringing my memoir to life.

# INDEX

The abbreviation RK = Ronni Kahn

United States, food rescue in
135–9
utopianism 47

Valentine's Day 85
verDuin Palit, Helen 136–41,
201, 223
Virgin Airlines 188
Vodafone World of Difference
program 198–9
volunteers 153–6, 208–9, 264,
282–5

Wallace, Kev 282–5
White, Julie 147–50, 157–8, 161,
163–4, 194
Witwatersrand University 37
women's refuges 73–5
Woolworths 204–5, 208

Yiddish 8, 198
yoga 170
Yom Kippur war 57–61